Designing for Newspapers and Magazines

Designing for Newspapers and Magazines examines how newspapers and magazines are produced. It offers guidance on how to produce attractive publications and how to tailor them to their target audience by advising on the use of colour, text placement, typography and images.

Designing for Newspapers and Magazines shows how a well designed publication can provide a powerful platform for good journalism. Written by an experienced journalist and designer, the book details the elements of good design and provides instruction on how to get the most out of computers and computer-aided design. A final section examines a range of different local and national publications and explains the reasoning that underpins their design choices.

Designing for Newspapers and Magazines includes:

- how to set up a new publication
- planning an edition of a newspaper or magazine
- typography and working with text
- working with images and technical production
- design pages and how to use colour
- design and journalism ethics
- a glossary of journalistic and design terms

Chris Frost is head of journalism at Liverpool John Moores University. He has worked in journalism for thirty years as reporter, sub-editor and editor. He is the author of *Media Ethics and Self-Regulation* and *Reporting for Journalists*.

Media Skills

SERIES EDITOR: RICHARD KEEBLE, CITY UNIVERSITY, LONDON
SERIES ADVISERS: WYNFORD HICKS AND JENNY MCKAY

The *Media Skills* series provides a concise and thorough introduction to a rapidly changing media landscape. Each book is written by media and journalism lecturers or experienced professionals and is a key resource for a particular industry. Offering helpful advice and information and using practical examples from print, broadcast and digital media, as well as discussing ethical and regulatory issues, *Media Skills* books are essential guides for students and media professionals.

Also in this series:

English for Journalists, 2nd edition
Wynford Hicks

Writing for Journalists
Wynford Hicks with Sally Adams and Harriett Gilbert

Interviewing for Radio
Jim Beaman

Producing for the Web
Jason Whittaker

Ethics for Journalists
Richard Keeble

Scriptwriting for the Screen
Charlie Moritz

Interviewing for Journalists
Sally Adams, with an introduction and additional material by Wynford Hicks

Researching for Television and Radio
Adèle Emm

Reporting for Journalists
Chris Frost

Find out more details of current *Media Skills* books and forthcoming titles at
www.producing.routledge.com

Designing for Newspapers and Magazines

Chris Frost

 Routledge
Taylor & Francis Group

LONDON AND NEW YORK

This book is dedicated to my family. Thanks to them for allowing me to use their pictures in various illustrations.

First published 2003 by Routledge
2 Park Square, Milton Park, Abingdon, Oxon OX14 4RN

Simultaneously published in the USA and Canada
by Routledge
270 Madison Avenue, New York, NY 10016

Reprinted 2005, 2007 (twice), 2008, 2009

Routledge is an imprint of the Taylor & Francis Group, an informa business

Typeset in Goudy Old Style and Syntax by
Keystroke, Jacaranda Lodge, Wolverhampton
Printed and bound in Great Britain by
the MPG Books Group

British Library Cataloguing in Publication Data
A catalogue record for this book is available from the British Library

Library of Congress Cataloging in Publication Data
has been applied for

ISBN 978–0–415–29026–5 (hbk)
ISBN 978–0–415–29027–2 (pbk)

Contents

Figures

1

Introduction

Newspapers and magazines are a potent mix of text and image designed to grab the reader's attention and hold it, making the experience of reading the news easy and enjoyable and, more importantly for some, to tempt readers to carry on shelling out a reasonable amount of precious cash to pay for it.

The aim of a magazine front cover or a newspaper front page is solely to invite the reader to buy, to tempt them into picking up the publication and become engrossed in its content. The aim of the inside is to continue that experience by offering information, education and entertainment.

The aim of this book is to look at how this is done both from the point of view of the student who seeks to know about publications and their ability to hold onto readership day after day, but also for the student or practitioner who wants to become a newspaper or magazine editor or designer and needs to know how this ambition is achieved.

Designing publications is part craft and part art. The craft of producing good publications that will attract readers can be taught, but, it has to be said, as with many things, talent is important and either one has the talent to produce good publication design or one hasn't. However, anyone can learn how to put together a sound and attractive publication with a bit of effort and practice. The average weekly paper, and particularly small newsletters and specialist publications are often at the very basic end of the design spectrum. There is usually only a small staff and these are often writers rather than designers.

The design of a publication is a delicate process. It is not possible to lay down fixed rules: first do this, then that. The good designer knows what is right and what is wrong, but often finds it very difficult to explain why this should be so.

Publication design involves a number of differing elements: headlines, body text, pictures, graphics, typefaces, white space and the technical limitations of the production process must all be thought about while following a publication's style and the fashion of the time, for the final element of any design is fashion. It is important to try new things, to keep a design fresh, but not so new that the publication appears too bizarre and puts potential readers off. Too traditional and the publication will appear old-fashioned, but too new and it will appear quirky and unappealing to many readers.

Because explaining design is difficult, this book tends to aim at technique. I start the next chapter by looking at the function of design and how it can help sell the publication and help the reader use the product.

Chapter 3 looks at publication style. All publications are designed to follow a certain style to help give it identity. A number of decisions are taken when a publication is first set up so that the publication has a particular look that will be easy to recognise, giving the publication a character all of its own. I look at these style choices and discuss the process and the likely decisions made.

Chapter 4 looks at the production process – printing. Printing has been with us for more than four hundred years, but it has limitations. There are things we can't do with printing and designers need to be aware of what these are. These limitations involve things such as the size of publication, the frequency of pub-lication and the speed at which we can publish. The Internet for instance (in theory at least) allows us to produce thousands of pages and publish them instantly, updating them as often as we like. The publication could also be any size. This is not an opportunity we have with printed material, but there are other advantages – newspapers and magazines are still the easiest media to access on the train or bus. If the good designer is aware of the printing process and how it works, a better quality product can be achieved.

Chapter 5 looks at the pre-planning process a designer needs to go through in order to set up an edition of a publication. How many pages will be needed, what will go on those pages and how are those decisions made?

Once the edition is planned, then the designer can look at individual pages and how they are best presented to give the reader the best experience. Designing pages involves making life easier for the reader, allowing him or her to find all the material on the page easily, making the task of reading the material as easy and as enjoyable as possible. A light-entertainment, coffee-break magazine should have easy-to-read pages with small snippets of information, easily tracked so that the reader feels he or she has had an entertaining experience. A serious broadsheet should also make it easy for the reader to find and read a serious column on the financial plight of Aids victims in Uganda, but this time there should be plenty of solid information presented in a way which minimises the task of reading thousands of heart-rending words.

After looking at structuring individual pages, in Chapter 7 I turn to discussing templates and style sheets. Most computer systems these days try to ease the designer's task by allowing the development of templates, which produce standardised pages and style sheets which pre-select the fonts required for that publication. These can make life a lot easier and so you should be aware of the part they can play in production.

Typography is the subject of Chapter 8. Type is the primary tool of a publication designer. What font you use, how it looks and how you use it will radically alter the look of a publication and will also vary the reader's experience. Choose the right font and the right size and the reading experience is effortless, make a bad choice and the reader may well give up without even realising why they found it such a strain.

Having looked at type, Chapter 9 discusses it as a display device – showing how we can use type as part of the design to draw the reader into the page and keep them there.

The other vital element in any publication are the images, whether these are photographs or graphics, or a mixture of the two. Pictures are a vital ingredient in telling any story and also help to form the style of a publication whether they are the page three girls of the *Sun*, the more serious-minded photographs of the *Guardian* or the traditionally posed interiors of *Hello!*. Chapter 10 looks at choosing pictures, at how you should crop them to suit the purpose for which they were chosen and how to go about scaling them to fit in the space available.

Colour has become very important to all publications over the past thirty years and is discussed in Chapter 11. Magazines have been using full colour for quite a long time now, twenty to thirty years. But newspapers have only really been using extensive colour since the late 1980s, following its introduction onto Fleet Street with the now defunct *Today*. Although at the time, some of the more traditional papers resisted introducing colour onto their pages, there is now hardly a newspaper in the land that does not use some colour and using it to maximum advantage has become an important element of design.

Chapter 12 looks at some of the ethical dilemmas of publishing and concentrates very specifically on the ethical dilemmas of design and editing, ignoring the more general ethical difficulties of journalism such as truth-telling, invading personal privacy and protecting people's reputations. As well as discussing copyright it also looks at the issues of taste and decency. How far can a publication go in producing material that might offend a reader? Is it legitimate to publish photographs of dead bodies or nudes, for instance?

Chapter 13 attempts to address the deficiency of the previous chapters which have all been largely about technique. This chapter analyses pages from newspapers and magazines to see how designers have tackled particular problems and found solutions or produced particularly attractive designs. It is an attempt at a masterclass where you will be invited to study the pages outlined in detail and be guided through what has been done to make those pages a success. Please try to examine these examples, as well as pages in every newspaper and magazine you come across from now on in order to see how good design is both unobtrusive but vital in giving the reader an entertaining and effortless reading experience.

At the end of the book you will find a glossary of technical terms and whenever a term in the glossary is used in the book, it will appear in italics to remind you that its meaning is explained in the glossary. There is also a bibliography which contains additional reading, together with one or two websites that are particularly useful.

2

The history and function of design

Before considering how to do something it is always worth thinking about why we do it. In this case, before deciding what makes a good design and how to go about achieving it, it is well worth considering why we spend the time, effort and expense required to produce good design.

THE PURPOSE OF GOOD DESIGN

Newspapers and magazines are carefully designed in order to present the journalism they contain in the clearest and most attractive way to the reader; the purpose of good design is to sell the journalism to the reader and make the act of consuming it as easy as possible.

Good design, whether for newspapers, cars or electric toasters, makes the product as easy to use as possible. A toaster might look very sleek, modern and easy to clean with the slots for the bread placed underneath, but having to juggle with a hot toaster in order to get the toast out would not make the design attractive to its users. I bought a new kettle recently, but although the model we favoured was by far the best looking, it did not have a measure to show the amount of water it contained. Consequently, we would have had to remove the lid and look inside before each use – a serious waste of time – and so the kettle was discarded as being too much like hard work.

Similarly, we might be smitten by the look of a 1950s chrome-plated classic car, but we would be unlikely to exchange it for our reliable, comfortable, easy-to-run modern hatchback, at least on a day-to-day basis. Good design can include looking attractive but it must also be convenient, easy to understand and helpful to the user.

NEWSPAPER DESIGN HISTORY

Newspapers and magazine design, like most things, is heavily affected by the available technology. Electrical goods of the 1930s and 1940s were angular in design because their cases had to be made of wood. Modern electrical goods, moulded from plastic, can be almost any shape the designer requires and so the shapes are often much rounder with a lot of detail. That said, of course, provided the container is essentially box shaped to hold the parts and prevent users from touching dangerous electrical terminals, it can be any shape and nowadays, many designers have gone 'retro' copying the squarer shapes of earlier years using wood or metal rather than plastic. Fashion also has a very definite part to play in design. The designer also needs to take into consideration that the item will be stored somewhere and so a flat base is essential to prevent the item rolling off tables or shelves.

Newspapers have been around since the early days of printing. A hundred years ago copy used to be run in single columns until the story ended. Another would then follow on immediately. Single column headings would run in *decks*; the only indication of the strength of the story being the number of decks. The headlines were usually straightforward:

THE WAR IN
THE CRIMEA

troops advance

a dispatch from

our correspondent

The technology at this stage made it difficult to produce a more sophisticated design, nor was there a need to. The people reading newspapers were from the middle classes who were anxious for news of domestic and world affairs. There was little need to entice them to buy a paper. In any case, before the invention of radio there was very little to entertain a person at home once the domestic duties had been completed. Some people played musical instruments, others read. Newspapers were a cheap and convenient method of providing information and entertainment.

The First World War saw the move into more elaborate display with the introduction of regular multi-column headings and banners in the *Express*. Most newspapers followed suit and started to use double-column headings, at least occasionally. Lower case was sometimes used but type sizes were still small in comparison with today, rarely larger than 36pt, according to Hutt (1967: 36). Newspapers also standardised on seven columns with measures of 14 or 13½ ems.

The transfer of the printing and publishing of the *Daily Herald* to Odhams, accomplished after much soul searching by the Trades Union Congress in 1929, and the subsequent publication of the *Odhams-Herald* in March 1930 was 'a technical sensation' (Hutt 1967: 38). At last a newspaper had been produced that was designed with strong headlines, clear shapes and a bold outlook. Still very much a paper of its time as viewed from today, it was a revelation for the period.

In 1933, Arthur Christiansen was appointed editor of the *Express*. Christiansen is seen by many observers as the most influential Fleet Street editor of all time and is certainly the most important in terms of design. Christiansen's choice of type and his move to more modern styles of headline writing turned the *Express* into the biggest selling daily paper of its time. In 1934, Harry G. Bartholomew turned the *Mirror* and the *Sunday Pictorial* into tabloids with big bold sans serif headings and large (for the time) picture spreads. The *Mirror*'s circulation rocketed, overtaking the *Express*, to become Britain's biggest selling daily news-paper – a position it held well into the 1980s, before it was overtaken by the *Sun*. The *Mirror* averaged sales of between 4.5 and 5.2 million throughout the 1950s and 1960s (Smith 1974: 97). This early *Mirror* was produced with four 15 em columns and it wasn't until the Second World War that the paper took up the seven 9 em columns that were the norm until very recently.

The *Daily Mail* was the next paper to radically change the way papers were designed. Editor Mike Randall and his production editor Leslie Sellers took a new approach in the mid-1960s with Randall seeking to free the *Mail* from the 'old restrictive orthodoxy' while Sellers introduced a streamlined, new style with lower case centralised splashes and new easier typefaces: Century Schoolbook for headings and Jubilee for the body text. At this stage the *Mail* was still *broadsheet*, but had a style that is still apparent in many a broadsheet provincial daily. Sellers may not have invented modern sub-editing, but he was certainly one of its biggest publicists and his two books on sub-editing (see bibliography) are still must-reads for all would-be sub-editors.

The next major change was technologically driven. Starting in the provinces in the 1970s, newspapers slowly moved over to web-offset production. This greatly improved the reproduction of photographs and type and newspapers were able to use much bigger pictures and display headings. The move to computer setting freed these papers from the fixed column and they gradually started to make their columns wider and use more *bastard* setting. Magazines had been using web-offset for some time, mainly to allow them to introduce more colour. They also moved over to computer setting faster than newspapers.

'Single key stroke' computer setting was a late introduction to the British publishing scene, but once introduced it quickly took over. Single key stroke setting, often called direct input, meant that reporters could type their stories directly into the computer and sub-editors would then edit them on screen. Under the traditional system, reporters had to type their stories on typewriters. The sub-editors then edited this 'hard copy' before sending it to the composing room to be set by the compositors. Proofreaders then checked the copy against the edited original to remove errors inserted into the text by the setters. The sub-editors then re-checked the work as it was placed onto pages on the *stone*.

Resistance to single keying came from the main printing union, the National Graphical Association (NGA) – the forerunner of today's General Print and Media Union – which feared that many of its compositor members would lose their livelihoods. It was the job of NGA members to re-enter material typed by members of the National Union of Journalists (NUJ) into the computer. The NGA had considerable power in the publishing industry because it operated closed shops and was not afraid to pull its members out on strike, preventing the publication in question from being printed. Because the NGA failed to reach agreement with publishers over the introduction of single keying, direct setting was not introduced into Britain until more than ten years after the USA.

Eventually an agreement was made between the NUJ (whose members would type and edit their stories directly into the new computer setting systems) and the NGA. Their 'direct entry' agreement allowed for the retraining of displaced NGA members as journalists in return for journalists being able to enter their stories directly into the computer system. The unions were then able to negotiate new technology agreements with the newspaper owners and computers were introduced. The agreements were made in 1986 and within five years, you would have been hard-pressed to find a newspaper that was not directly set on computer.

This combination of direct setting and web-offset printing was soon followed by computer systems capable of making up pages on screen so that all the setting and design work could be done on screen with the plates for the press being produced directly from a plate-making machine attached to the computer. Today, even photographs are now digitally produced allowing them to be sent over telephone networks and inserted directly onto computer-set pages.

This new direct-set technology allowed for considerable freedom of design as editors no longer had to work within the old restraints of the hot-metal setting machines (linotypes) and the rigid columns they required.

This new freedom was developed by the introduction of colour presses in the late 1980s. Driven by advertisers' demands, magazines had been printing in full colour since the mid-1970s. But the extra time the process involved meant that newspapers had not done more than use *spot colour*.

The newest presses allowed the use of full colour on several of the pages in the modern newspaper including the front and back. This allowed newspapers to add colour to their designs and the newspaper as we know it today started to roll off the press. Although many of the daily papers resisted its introduction, feeling that it would add nothing and indeed, in the case of some of the more serious broadsheets, would trivialise what they were offering, all national newspapers and most provincial ones were printing in full colour on some pages at least, by the mid-1990s.

THE IMPORTANCE OF BRAND

The look, size and shape of a publication has an important impact on the way it is viewed by the reader. In an age when brand is all important and designer labels determine which consumer items we buy, how the publication is marketed and its design is an important consideration. The *Daily Star* is aimed at a youthful, male market while the *Daily Mail* seeks a more sober, aspiring, female audience; middle class, middle-aged and middle England; *Cosmopolitan* is after a younger, less-traditional but still female audience while the *Oldie* aims for those seeking to relax in their autumn years. It doesn't take more than a quick scan of a newspaper or magazine to spot the audience it is seeking both by considering the type of stories it is using and by how it displays them.

This brand image is as important for a publication as it is for any other product in today's retail-dominated lifestyle. In an age where many people describe their favourite leisure-time activity as shopping, publications need to be one of the things people shop for.

The first job of any new production editor is to reconsider the publication's target audience and to assess whether its audience identifies with the brand presented.

DESIGNERS AND SUBS

Newspaper and magazine designers come from several different sorts of backgrounds. Generally, provincial newspaper designers are journalists. They are sub-editors with sufficient seniority and experience to design and manage individual pages while the chief sub or production editor will design and manage the entire edition. In magazines and national newspapers, journalists control what goes onto each page and manage the entire edition, but it is often a graphic designer who will actually design the page and put it together on screen. Magazine pages usually have more complex designs than newspaper pages and integrate graphics, photographs and text more closely. Although newspapers often have quite sophisticated designs in supplements and feature pages, the news pages are simpler, more modular and more likely to be produced to a standardised template. This is because speed is the most important factor for news pages and the opportunities for sophisticated design are limited, while the journalistic decision making is paramount.

In a typical provincial evening newspaper the production team is led by the production editor or chief sub-editor. This executive answers directly to the editor for the way the newspaper looks. The editor, news editor, chief photographer and chief sub-editor meet every day to discuss what news is to go in the paper and how it should look. This gives the chief sub the chance to discuss with the other executives what stories are being considered, how significant they are for the target audience, how much copy there is likely to be and whether there are suitable pictures.

For instance, the conference might hear that there has been a bad house blaze over night. The news editor would inform the conference that a reporter is writing up a basic report on the fire and the two dead and three injured involved. Other reporters have been instructed to:

- get a condition report on the family who lived in the house;
- track down relatives of the family for information about them and to get pictures;
- talk to neighbours to find out what happened in detail.

The chief photographer will report on the pictures obtained at the scene and any other photographs available. There might be a picture of one of the family members concerned in the newspaper's library, for instance.

The editor might then decided to make the story the front page splash with further reports and pictures going inside the paper. It will then be the chief sub's job to ensure those pages contain the appropriate copy and pictures.

The editor might also decide to instruct the features editor to assign a reporter to find out more for the next day's edition as there have been several fires in that area in the last few months, with one previous death. Is it coincidence? Is something else going on?

In smaller weekly papers or magazines, the team might be smaller, with one person doing several of the jobs outlined above, but the basic process would be the same. Even on a magazine so small that there is only an editor, that person will need to go through the same process of considering what is available, what more is needed and how everything can be put together to make a suitable experience for the reader.

For a large magazine however, it would be the art editor and his or her team who would be responsible for designing the pages, drawing together the text, pictures and graphics into an attractive package.

3
Publication style

When a publication is first set up, a lot of design decisions need to be made that will set the style for publication. Once a publication is up and running, it is important that it continues to present a familiar face to its audience and that it has a clear identity that will suit its target audience. Readers should be able to recognise a publication easily and identify with it. There is often an aspirational nature to a publication's style. People don't read *Vogue* because they are cool, hip, trendsetting style-leaders, but because they would like to be thought of as cool, hip, trendsetting style-leaders who mix easily with the stars at fashionable parties. If they feel they are (or want to be) young, cool, hip and up with the latest fashions, then that is the image the publication should present. If, by contrast, the target audience of a publication includes people who are comfortable with their lives, who like things to stay the same and are conservative, at least by nature if not politics, then again this is what publication should reflect. The modern publication needs to be up-to-the-minute, while still maintaining an identifiable style. The traditional publication needs to appear unchanging and classic, without being boring and dull – even those who want to relax in comfort want to read something that will interest them!

The trick is done by thinking carefully about how the publication will look from issue to issue and how the design will allow the publication to have a distinctive identity without always appearing the same. It's a trick all successful publications achieve. The *Daily Mail* is good at it – get hold of a couple of copies produced several weeks apart and see how there is a clear identity that a reader can easily spot on the newsstand, without each issue appearing to be an identikit of the other. See Figure 13.1 which shows a *Daily Mail* front page with its traditional style of headline font, bold use of pictures and a clear modular structure.

Although this book is aimed at journalists working on newspapers and magazines where the house style will already have been decided, you may well be called upon to start a new publication for a company who wants to send its staff an internal newsletter, or you may end up producing a highly specialised newsletter for a society or business. I have tried to bear this in mind while writing this chapter.

TARGET AUDIENCE

The first consideration when designing any publication is the audience at which it is aimed. The whole style of the publication will vary depending on who is to read it and why.

A magazine aimed at providing young women with entertainment while they relax will be entirely different to a booklet aimed at providing detailed product information to a busy purchasing officer in a large company.

You need to think carefully about the target audience and its needs. There is often a temptation to say that a publication needs to be read by everybody, but this is never true. There will always be a target audience. This could be based on geography, demographics, interest, work, school or college. Even a local weekly newspaper that is aimed at the whole community is only bought by a certain sector, or at least a certain sector for certain purposes. There is not enough space here for an in depth discussion of who buys and reads newspapers, but a quick look at the local newspaper will show up certain distinct markets. Readers buy the newspaper because they:

- are interested in the local community (including looking at births, marriages and deaths);
- are looking for a new job;
- want to buy a house or a car;
- follow local sport;
- are looking for rented accommodation or have some other interest in the small ads;
- want to know about local events and 'what's on';
- had their attention caught by an interesting-looking local story on the front page;
- find the paper an interesting read that helps them relax at home.

Although each of these groups will buy the newspaper, not all of them are likely to be affected by the design. Those seeking jobs, cars, houses, and so on are likely to buy the paper regardless of design. Those with a serious interest in their local community probably have the paper ordered from their local newsagent and would only cancel the paper because the standards had become atrocious, and maybe not even then.

The only groups likely to base their decision to buy on the design of the paper are those in the last two categories. However, those who buy for the ads are likely to stop buying once their demands have been met and again good design and an interesting read may mean they would stick with the paper. So the design does not need to aim at everybody, only those likely to buy the paper on impulse from a newsagent, newsstand or that latest and most important newsseller, the local garage.

USAGE

Another consideration to bear in mind when designing a publication from scratch is what will happen to the publication once the reader has bought it. The reader will take it from the shelf (or the letterbox if it's a subscription) and flick through it. What happens then?

We need to consider how the reader will read the publication, when they will read it and what they will do with it once they've finished reading it.

How the reader will read the publication depends on what it is. A newspaper is read fairly soon after it is bought. You don't buy a newspaper to read a week later (although you might keep the occasional article or supplement in order to read later or to show someone else). Newspapers, whether bought at a shop or newsstand or delivered, are read while commuting, on a break from work, or at home in the evening, often while watching television. Once they are read, they might be passed on to someone else or they are thrown in the bin to be recycled as packaging or kitty litter.

They therefore need to be cheap and easy to recycle (so that throwing away is acceptable) and they do not need to be stored. Storing large-sized publications such as newspapers is not as easy as storing small-sized ones (A5). However, larger sizes (A2 or A3) do not require sophisticated (and expensive) binding.

Tabloids are generally preferred by readers because they do not require the arm-stretch of a gorilla to read them. While this is not the main reason that tabloids are more popular, it is certainly one of them. However, since tabloids limit how much can be written on one story and since requiring readers to turn pages to follow stories is a bad idea, those papers that carry more in depth journalism prefer broadsheets.

Whether your paper is tabloid or broadsheet we have to understand that storage of such newspapers is not easy, which is one reason why libraries go to the trouble and expense of putting them on microfilm.

Newspapers are cheap because of the production methods they are able to use. Relatively cheap newsprint is used and it is printed in a way that limits expensive technical processes. If newspapers had to be trimmed more carefully, cut, folded and bound they would be much more expensive and would probably not be economically viable.

Consumer magazines, on the other hand, are very different. The typical monthly magazine is designed to be kept for at least a month. It is not expected that you would read it in an hour or so and then get rid of it. It is designed to be read over several sessions. This means that you will need to store the magazine somewhere – a coffee table, a magazine rack or down the side of the sofa. Either way, the publication needs to be more robust than a newspaper. The paper needs to be tougher and better able to stand up to a lot of handling. There might be a light card cover to help stiffen and protect the contents. The quality of printing is much higher than that of newspapers. Magazines are usually fully printed in colour which requires a very white paper for maximum effectiveness. They also need to be relatively easy to store, while still being as cheap as possible. This means that a much thicker, higher quality of white paper is used that is bonded (laminated with a plastic) to keep the ink in place and to repel sticky fingers, coffee and other accidents of every-day life. Magazines are normally of A4 size, because this balances the cost of dealing with a large number of pages with ease of storage. However a number of women's magazines have recently started experimenting with smaller sizes closer to A5, claiming this will allow the reader to keep the magazine in her handbag. It is interesting to note this new storage imperative – the handbag rather than a briefcase or the kitchen table. Some of the men's magazines are now following this example, although one presumes that handbag storage is not the main reason.

The point about many consumer magazines is that the reader may want to keep them – often for years. Keen hobbyists will find there are several magazines to support them these days whether they are keen on collecting teddy bears, fishing or surfing the Internet. All carry reviews and how-to-do-it style articles and the hobbyist will want to keep these on his or her shelf. An A4 or A5 sort of size is ideal for this kind of storage. Of course book publishers tend to stick with a size near to A5 because bookshelves, whether in a library or at home, are designed for that sort of size. Book-size is easy to handle and to store. Books stand upright easily without collapsing under their own weight and they are easy to carry about. Occasionally a book is published that is larger than A4 size, but this is fairly rare and is usually limited to books containing pictures that need to be a certain size.

Ultimately it is always budget that limits the main features of a publication. Additional money is only spent on higher quality of magazines because publishers know that without it, the magazine would not sell well. A publication's design always needs to consider the budget and whether the spending can be justified by the potential sales.

COLOUR

One of the first things to affect budget is colour. Printing in a single colour is always cheapest. Usually black ink on white paper is used, although it isn't necessarily so. Ink comes in a huge range of shades. Paper similarly comes in a number of shades. However, white paper and black ink are by far the cheapest and are certainly the easiest to read. If cost transcends any other consideration, then print black on white.

If the budget is tight, but not that tight, then it is worth considering coloured paper or coloured ink. Usually this is best considered if you wish to use two colours of ink (*spot colour*). This will allow you to print the main text in black, but put the occasional headline, caption or other piece of text in a different colour. This is relatively cheap, much cheaper than *process colour* (full photographic-style representative colour). Once you go past two colours of ink however, it's often as cheap to go for full colour.

PAPER

The type of paper can vary enormously, as can its cost. Visit the sales room of a new luxury housing estate and pick up a sales brochure. No nasty newsprint here. The brochure is likely to be printed in full colour on high quality art paper of the sort artists use for water colours. Thick and stiff, it might be separated from the next page by a light page of tracing paper; all highly luxurious and very expensive. The builder has spent a lot on printing knowing that the only way to sell luxury homes is with luxury brochures. Penny pinching here would be a waste of money. *Private Eye* can use cheap newsprint for its fortnightly publication, because its readership is not only not concerned with quality, but would actually be suspicious of such a magazine were it printed in full colour and on high quality paper; they would accuse it of having sold out.

PAGINATION

The number of pages and the balance between editorial content and advertising is another budgetary consideration. Pages cost money to produce and so need to be supported by the income produced by advertising. The calculation of ad rates and percentages of adverts to editorial content is really outside the scope of this book, but journalists certainly need to be aware of the impact of income on pagination. A free newspaper that relies solely on advertising for income can have as little as 20 per cent of its space devoted to editorial. Even a paid for newspaper may have as little as one third of its overall space devoted to editorial.

TECHNICAL DATA

Once basic decisions have been taken about the way a publication should look, its size, style and shape, more detailed decisions have to be made about how each page will look.

The size of the margins, headers and footers, artwork and the number of columns used will all effect the publication's appearance and how the reader will react to it. Try going in to a large newsagent and look at all the different publications: newspapers, consumer magazines, specialist weeklies and so on. Look quickly at the size and style and then see how each page is presented. All will differ from each other, but all will have been chosen to look as they do to be as attractive as possible to their potential readers.

Margins

Most newspapers are obliged to have margins around the page as part of the printing process. The machines that print newspapers are designed to run a large number of copies very quickly. Margins allow for there to be a certain amount of leeway about exactly where the fold and the centre margins go and where the edges of the pages are cut.

Magazines these days are not normally run off at such speed and are printed in much higher quality both in terms of colour and the quality of paper. Magazines therefore can be 'bled' so that the ink runs over the edge of the notional page size leaving it flush with the edge of the page after the magazines have been trimmed by an enormous and powerful guillotine during the production process.

Newspapers want to waste the minimum margin space so these are normally set very narrow as is the space between columns, called the *gutter*.

Page structure

The next decision to be made is about the structure of the page. Should it be run into columns, if so how many, and should the column widths be rigidly adhered to? There are two main considerations here. The first is the legibility of the print and the difference column width makes to the speed of reading. The second concerns the effect the number of columns have on the reader in terms of design.

Research suggests (Tinker and Paterson cited in Tinker 1963: 78) that a 10pt solid (unspaced) line of type is read most easily if it is between 19 picas (8.045 cm) and 32 picas (13.55 cm) wide (picas are a measurement for type – see Chapter 8 for a full description). Type with more space between the lines becomes easier to read. However, in another study, it was found that 8pt type set solid was best read in lines of 13 picas to 25 picas (Tinker: 1963). It seems that the smaller the type, the narrower the column can be. Using the examples given by Tinker, we can see (not too surprisingly), that we read best if there are at least eight words per line and no more than 19 words per line. Since newspapers traditionally have narrower columns and are often read in less than ideal conditions (all Tinker's experiments were carried out in ideal conditions) then a narrower column width might be acceptable. Being jogged around on a commuter train is likely to make a reader lose his or her place more easily, a narrow column should make it easier to find the place again.

Most normal newspaper columns of 8 pica-ems in a tabloid and 10 to 11 pica-ems for a broadsheet are too narrow to allow readers to make maximum use of their peripheral vision (Tinker 1963: 80) even when the type is set in 8pt (a normal size for newspapers). Many modern newspapers have increased their column widths in recent years to cope with this problem. Computer setting and modern methods have made this much easier to do. The tradition of narrow columns still exists however, and many editors stick to seven or eight columns because that is the way newspapers are 'supposed to look'. The *Guardian* for instance still runs eight columns across its news pages. Many tabloid papers however are running much wider columns and the *Daily Mirror*, *Sun* and *Daily Mail* rarely have more than five columns on their news pages.

Many newspapers vary the number of columns between pages so that feature pages may have wider columns than news pages. This is because features are usually longer than news and it makes sense to sacrifice the busy, active look of narrow columns for a more leisurely and straightforward read for a longer feature piece. The *Guardian*, for instance, in its feature supplements chooses a standard five columns so that even though the pages are tabloid, the columns are significantly wider than news pages.

It is also possible to move away from the traditional, rigid approach that demands that news pages should have a particular number of columns to a freer approach that allows the number of columns to be varied from page to page or even within a page. This is easy to do nowadays but without computer setting in the days of hot metal, this was not the case. Today, many newspapers will vary the number of columns down a page depending on what stories and pictures they want to use. This is known as *bastard* setting. I'm not sure whether this is because it used to be hard to do or because it was seen as something improper, however it is widely practised these days and newspapers tend to look the better for it.

Magazines have never been as tightly structured as newspapers. Again the width of columns is open to debate, but magazines tend to use *bastard* setting as a norm.

There might be a vague feeling that there should be three or four columns per page and over-narrow or over-wide columns should be avoided, at least for any length of text, but otherwise magazine design is pretty free these days.

The only other consideration, when it comes to columns, is whether there should be an even or odd number. In practical terms it probably makes little difference, but having an even number can lead to the temptation of making pages that are too symmetrical and risk breaking the page into a number of subsections. Sometimes, of course, this may be the effect that's wanted, but generally a page is designed to present the reader with an entire shape and an odd number of columns is often easier to work with.

It is also worth mentioning at this point that facing pages should really be designed as pairs. Often (in newspapers at least) this is not the case unless the pages are a *spread* specifically designed to work as a pair. However, where possible it is wise to design facing pages together (deadlines often mean this is not possible). Research from the Poynter Institute (Garcia and Stark 1991: 30) shows that that is how the reader deals with them, whether we design them individually or not.

House style

House style is an important element to think about when designing a new publication.

If you are producing the work for a corporate customer, they may already have a house style, a certain font they always use, a colour or colours that always appear on their documents. If you are dealing with a customer who has never produced such work, you may need to discuss with them what fonts, colours and logos they intend to use throughout the publication.

The importance of a house style cannot be overestimated. Just think how often you have identified the source of material just by the way it looks. The way a publication looks tells the world about the company that produced it, so how it looks is very important. Showing that you are lively and go ahead, or honest and reliable can all be done in the type used to produce the publication, the paper colour and the colours used for the text. Virgin's brash, go-ahead image is underlined by its use of bright red and its distinctive script, signature-style logo. The Beatles will always be identified, even by people who were not born until 20 years later, by the distinctive serif font caps used for their name.

The first selection you need to make is a choice of colour. This can be fixed in your DTP software to ensure that you always produce material to the house style. Fonts also need to be chosen and loaded onto the publication. A font can say a lot about a customer and should be chosen with care.

Logos are also important and if a customer has not yet got a logo, they should be guided to a suitable graphic designer. If they already have a logo, get a copy to scan into their publications.

Type

Just as there is a house style for colours and fonts, there is also a house style for the way you use the text. What font should you use. Should it run justified or ragged left? Do you use bold? What is the headline style?

Most newspapers and magazines tend to call in specialist consultants when it comes to setting up the designs (or redesigns) of newspapers and magazines. They will balance the technical requirements of a newspaper's font against the design requirements.

Some of the elements they will consider are the legibility of the type. They will want to be sure readers can read it easily. They will check that it prints well and looks good after printing. Provided the font performs well in these technical areas, the designer will then want to know that it presents the style of image the publication wants. There are thousands of fonts, and it is difficult when looking at many of them to really spot the difference in the way they look, but the font will change the way people view that particular publication and reinforce the general image the newspaper seeks to present. That is particularly true of the chosen headline font which thrusts its way into people's view, but even the body type carries an image, because even though it is a lot more subtle, there is a lot more of it.

There are also purely commercial considerations. A font might carry the right image and be highly legible, but if it takes 20 per cent more space to carry the same number of words, then that might not be acceptable. Readers like to believe they are getting value for money and they are more likely to read a magazine that carries more on its pages, provided everything else is equal.

Graphics and photographs

Even graphics and photographs are run in a house style. This may be to have a one-point black border, or it could be to fade out the edges. There will also need to be some consideration of size of pictures and perhaps numbers of pictures per page.

Titlepiece

You also need to consider the *titlepiece* for a publication. This is the publication's name and is a crucial piece of the marketing jigsaw. The titlepiece is the presentation of the brand name and a lot of effort is taken over this design although the story goes that the *Sun*'s famous and simple logo was designed by Rupert Murdoch on the back of a napkin over dinner shortly after taking over the ailing broadsheet that was soon to become Britain's brightest and brashest tabloid. The *Sun*'s logo sums up everything the *Sun* represents: simple, straightforward, uncluttered and easy to read; brash and bright and very definitely in your face.

Unusually for the time, it was also set in the top left-hand quadrant of the page, allowing the right-hand to be used for *puffs* or *blurbs*, the pitches newspapers use to draw readers inside.

The *Daily Telegraph*'s titlepiece is also an ideal brand mark, recognisable well before the word becomes readable. Its use of an Old English-style font, set across most of the width of the page, is very traditional and classic, drawing on all the virtues the *Telegraph* hopes to represent.

Headers and footers

Every page of a publication carries the title of the publication, a page number and a date. Publications also need to decide how to present this. Subtle with a small font? Large, with a border? The choices are varied and again this will be designed by the consultant who sets up the paper design. These days, it is usually built into the page templates produced for use on the computer system, often Macintoshes using Quark Xpress.

Imprint

Last but not least, you need to ensure the imprint is included somewhere in the publication. The imprint says who printed and published the document and this is a legal requirement. Often it is put on the back page in very small type, but some publications make a virtue of it by putting it in a column that includes staff names and job titles. A magazine will usually list the staff and give phone numbers and contact e-mails. Many newspapers are also starting to follow this pattern realising that it is a good way to get readers to send in stories or make contact if something newsworthy is happening. Newspapers usually list the news desk, sports desk and advertising team with numbers and e-mails.

Colours

The colours to be used in a publication also help to build the publication's image and brand. Coca-Cola's bright red is a central component of its image, and in a similar way, various publications use particular colours to identify themselves. Using full colour for adverts and editorials might seem to suggest that there should be no limit to the colours used and this would be true for the content, however, on the masthead, imprint and regular logos and page headings, careful use of colour can make a distinctive addition to the brand. In some newspapers, not every page is set in colour and so you need to be aware that colour might not run throughout. In magazines these days, it is normal for all pages to be in colour, however there are plenty of small publication magazines or newsletters that use a limited amount of colour or rely more heavily on *spot colour* (see Chapter 4) and here specific colours can be used to give an identity.

4

Production processes

Design is largely about working with the technology available to you. Print is a fixed, two-dimensional medium with limited opportunities for colour. Most of this is visual and we aim publications at the sense of sight. Touch, smell and taste could be considered, but the technology is expensive and probably not worth it for most publications – although from time to time some magazines do carry adverts from scent manufacturers who do think it worth the money to produce scented adverts. It would also be technically possible to produce print with taste or texture, and even sound (birthday cards are now available with small sound devices that cheer or jeer as you open the card) although whether it would be worth the expense for a newspaper is doubtful. Magic pictures that move, such as those in the Harry Potter stories are yet to grace newspapers although *Press Gazette* did publish a 3D picture in summer 2002 and provided readers with the special glasses to view it. As designers then, the technology of print and what we can do with it is very important to us and so we need to know what is available so we can work out how to get the best from it.

PRINTING TECHNOLOGY

Making the most of print technology (as with all technology) is about balancing what is possible at the present stage of development with cost. Newspapers are produced at the cheaper, throwaway end of the market using cheap paper, cheap binding methods and limited colour reproduction. Magazines tend to be higher up the expense range with good quality paper and full colour throughout. The time taken to do something is also a cost. Since experiments and new ideas always take up more time than established practice, the gains have to be carefully weighed against the cost.

The good publication designer should always consider ways of being imaginative and creative, while remaining within budget. Usually of course, the publication is already pre-designed and you are obliged to work within the production limits, but that doesn't mean that you can't try out new things from time to time. Just because your publication is of a certain size, for instance, does that mean you are stuck with it? Who invented the gatefold or the pop-up book?

PRINTING PROCESSES

Printing started in earnest around the 1450s. Although wood blocks had long been used to reproduce copies of drawings and even type, the process was difficult and expensive. It was easier to get someone to copy the books by hand and while the church had monks employed solely at copying, the educated classes had to employ scribes to do the copying for them. Gutenberg's invention of moveable type and an ink suitable to use with it brought together several technologies to launch printing as we know it.

History of printing technology

The origins of print are difficult to determine as a number of ideas and processes needed to come together in order for it to be possible. Just as the computer could not be invented before electricity was discovered and tamed, so printing could not be considered until all the necessary elements came together in the same place at the same time.

The Chinese were significantly instrumental in the development of printing. They had invented paper by AD 105, replacing vellum and skins for the production of documents, thereby reducing their cost and so increasing their availability. The Romans invented inscribed lettering with the generally accepted date of AD 114 for the inscription at the base of Trajan's Column in Rome. The design of type lettering as opposed to script was an important development towards printing as it allowed a standardised alphabet to be reproduced.

Printing was developed during the first millennium and the legendary date of its inception is AD 594 although the oldest extant publication is the Diamond Sutra which bears the statement that it was printed on 11 May 868 (AD) by Wang Chieh. This was done with carved wood blocks.

Moveable type was the next thing that had to be invented before printing could develop significantly, although even this was not enough in itself. Moveable type was invented in China around 1040, but because it was of complicated Chinese ideographs, it did not take off. It was made from clay, baked hard.

Moveable copper type was cast in Korea in the early fifteenth century, but it was Johann Gensfleisch zur Laden known as Gutenberg (b. c.1399, d. 1468) who is credited with making the first press to use moveable type. He also invented an ink suitable for use with the new metal type.

Several of Gutenberg's works still survive. The Gutenberg bible (the forty-two-line bible) was published in Mainz probably by Gutenberg and his two associates Fust and Schoffer. It was probably begun in 1453 and completed in 1455. Printing in those days was not fast. The three associates fell out when Fust and Schoffer sued Gutenberg for the money they had lent him to set up his press. As is so often the case with inventors, Gutenberg was buried poor.

The press changed little over the next three hundred years with the initial inventions being consolidated 'in a predominately conservative way' (Steinberg 1955: 18). It says much of Gutenberg's achievement that while others improved on his ability as a printer, they did little to improve on the effectiveness of his press. Gutenberg could have walked into a press of 1720 and not only felt at home, but started work without problems. Within fifteen years of Gutenberg's death presses had been set up in every country of Western Christendom. Newspapers started during the 1600s with the first daily newspaper starting in England in 1702 as the *Daily Courant*.

As printing became more widespread, the need for some standardisation became accepted. Fournier le Jeune had proposed a unit as early as 1737 but it was Didot who introduced the point system in 1775 which was adopted throughout France and later in Germany. The system related the body size of the type to the then legal measurement, 'pied du roi', the size of the royal foot. A different system is used in the US and Britain today.

At the start of the nineteenth century, the trade started growing, fed by demand for more reading material from a public that was becoming more educated.

In 1798 mechanical methods of paper production were introduced. Paper costs plummeted by a quarter or even a third. Nicolas-Louis Robert invented a machine for making a continuous sheet of paper on an endless wire web. The patents were bought by the Fourdrinier brothers in 1804 and they developed it to make the first paper-making machines (Twyman 1970: 49).

Stereotyping was invented at the turn of the century and the patent was bought in this country by Lord Stanhope. Stereotyping allowed far more copies to be made more cheaply. Type is set into a frame known as a forme. Before stereotyping, the paper was then pressed onto the type which eventually became too worn or damaged to be used and the forme would need to be reset. By taking a plaster or papier mâché cast of the forme of type and then casting a new forme from this, reprints could be made without resetting.

Stanhope improved the press in 1804, exchanging the traditional wooden bed for an iron one and adapting the lever mechanism to allow the printing of a large forme in one pull instead of the old two pulls (Twyman 1970: 51).

These developments were quickly followed by steam-powered presses, patented by Koenig in 1810 (ibid.). No longer would man-power be the driving force behind the press. A technological evolution was taking place which was to revolutionise the press.

In 1812 Koenig built his first cylinder printing machine to take advantage of the reels of paper now available from the newly invented paper-making machines. The forme was still a flatbed but a cylinder now ran the paper over it. Its worth was soon appreciated when *The Times* adopted it in 1814. The print run improved from 300 sheets an hour to 1,100.

The four cylinder press, invented by Augustus Applegath and Edward Cowper, some fourteen years later raised printing speeds to 4,000 copies per hour for *The Times* (ibid.).

It was Edward Cowper who had the idea to curve stereotype plates in order to fasten them to a cylinder. This beginning of the rotary press was significant, but its time was yet to come. Cylinder presses, with the paper being pulled across the forme before being pressed and then driven on and cut free from the web, were still seen as the way ahead for financial reasons.

Rowland Hill patented a rotary press in 1835 but its advantages were nullified by the necessity of printing the duty-paid stamp onto each newspaper. Newspapers of the time were still obliged to pay stamp duty and the authorities would not allow this to be stamped on a continuous web of paper.

The Philadelphia Ledger introduced a rotary press shortly after this, although this machine did not use stereotypes. Formes of type were affixed to a horizontal central cylinder by means of tapering column rules.

In 1863, William Bullock patented his rotary self-feeding and self-perfecting press (able to print on both sides of the paper simultaneously) (ibid: 55) for use with curved stereos cast from a papier mâché impression of the original (a flong). This was built in 1865 and installed in the *Times* in 1866 printing 12,000 sections an hour. A folding mechanism was added in 1868. By 1939, the *Times* was printing a 32-page paper at a rate of 40,000 copies an hour.

1879 saw the introduction of a patent 'Auxiliary printing mechanism for Late News'. This printing device, allowed late news to be added to the front or back page without stopping the press. It meant that newspapers could carry the latest news even as they were being printed, although the amount of space available was limited to about a half column. This system was widely used by newspapers until very recently when the introduction of web-offset litho machines made its use impossible.

All this change throughout the 1800s brought in dramatic social changes. Rather than threaten jobs and wages, as had been feared, the increase in printing found a ready market in the newly educated. The growth of literacy meant that printers started making their money through printing larger runs. Before this, the money had been made in the composition rather than the printing because after printing a few thousand copies, the forme would need to be re-set as the type would be worn away. Stereos ensured the ability to cast new formes, and high speed presses meant long runs could be contemplated. Type casting had also come under the scrutiny of the inventor.

The first type-casting machine was invented in 1805 in the US by William Wing. But it was eventually abandoned. Another machine was invented by Anthony Francis Berte where a mould would be pressed against an aperture in the metal pot and hot metal squirted through under pressure. Many more variations were invented over the subsequent years and were received with mixed reactions.

Attempts to introduce typecasting machinery in Britain in 1823 met with a hostile reception from trades unions, although a similar machine invented in America by Dr William Church improved the number of letters cast from 3–7,000 a day to 12–20,000. Other composing machines were invented by Robert Hattersley (1866) and Charles Kastenbein (1869). Hattersley's machine was used by the UK provincial press until 1891 and Kastenbein's at the London *Times* until 1908 (Steinberg 1955: 196). Both machines needed manual justification and distribution of the type. This was so expensive that juvenile labour was used, a practice opposed by the London Society of Compositors, forerunner of today's Graphical Print and Media Union (GPMU). Only the non-union *Times* was prepared to oppose the union and used children to set type.

Ottmar Merganthaler invented the Linotype machine and it was installed in the *New York Tribune* in 1886 (ibid.). It was quickly taken up elsewhere, and nearly all newspapers in the twentieth century used the machines until quite recently. Doubtless many newspapers are still produced by this method, particularly in the third world where circulations can be large and where cost is paramount.

The linotype works by bringing together pieces of brass engraved with the type to be used in a line at the command of the operator's keyboard, automatically spaced and this brass line impressed on a line of hot lead-based metal to produce a slug of type. The brass matrices are then returned to the channels of a magazine for re-use. Monotype machines developed this process in 1889 casting each letter separately allowing easier correction. The ability to cast shot up from 2,000 letters an hour to around 6,000.

In 1891, the *Birmingham Daily Gazette* used electricity to drive a single roll press – the first British paper to use electricity. In 1906 Washington I. Ludlow invented the Ludlow machine for casting large sizes of type. It was introduced in England in 1911.

In 1882 the first practicable photographic halftone process for letterpress printing was patented in Munich and was introduced into England two years later by the Meisenbach company. The use of photographs in publications was developed for printing by the invention of the cross line screen that allowed halftone photography. This process allowed for the mechanical engraving of fine screen blocks and the printing of photographs in publications became financially possible.

With mechanical setting, photo-engraving, web-feeds and the power-driven self-perfecting rotary press, newspapers were set to produce for a mass market of the newly literate and the great newspaper days were born.

Until the 1800s all printing had been relief printing – the image was made by pressing a raised inked original onto paper.

Lithography – a non-relief printing method – had been invented in 1798 by the Bavarian Aloys Senefelder and this became more widely used later in the eighteenth century, particularly with the development of photography. It produced higher quality images but was a much more difficult process.

Photogravure – another new method of printing – was invented around 1890 with the first successful prints in 1895. This was also a non-relief method but required detailed engraving of the plate and so was difficult and expensive to set up. Once a plate had been engraved however, it would print very long runs making the cost per copy very low. This was to become the standard method of printing long runs of high quality colour work.

1904 saw the first commercial development of offset lithography and this was followed in 1925 by the first tentative moves to photocomposition with the prototype of a machine called the Uhertype (Twyman 1970: 63) introduced by Edward Uher, a Hungarian engineer. This was developed in 1929 with the introduction in America of a photosetting machine with a claimed 7,000 letters an hour.

1945 saw the first principles of Xerography and Xero-printing patented in America quickly followed in 1946 by the installation of the first effective photosetter in the Government printing office in Washington. The Harris-Intertype Fotosetter was used to produce the first fully filmset book – *Handbook of Basic Microtechnique*.

In the same way that the turn of the nineteenth century was a period of almost frantic change in the world of newspaper publishing, so the 1960s, 1970s and 1980s represent a massive technological revolution. The early part of the twentieth century had been taken up with world wars and any changes had been largely improvements on existing technology. Most newspapers were happy to use technology that had been largely unchanged since 1900. Fast rotary presses driven by electricity and supported by mechanical setting were adjusted with only such minor amendments as using plastic stereotypes rather than papier mâché.

The 1960s and 1970s now saw some rapid development. Photographic methods of typesetting, reproduction and printing led to vast improvements and halftone lithography was developed to a commercially acceptable standard. The first web-offset litho presses were installed during the 1960s. Multiweb presses were introduced and speeds were reached that had previously been undreamed of.

Photocomposition was introduced during the late 1960s and 1970s and by the end of the 1970s, many provincial daily papers were producing photoset artwork which was then photographically converted into plates to be loaded onto either the new web-offset presses or converted into stereotypes for traditional relief printing.

Direct input was introduced into newspapers in America throughout the late 1970s and early 1980s. This meant that the reporter's copy was no longer re-set by a compositor into the traditional metal or photoset type but was set directly on computer by the reporter. Fears of job losses from the National Graphical Association (NGA) ensured that direct setting was not introduced in Britain at all until much later. The *Nottingham Evening Post* started using the method in the early 1980s but remained virtually alone until Eddie Shah introduced it at his Warrington plant in 1984. This was followed by the launch of *Today* in 1985 and the move to Wapping by Rupert Murdoch in 1986.

Provincial newspapers began to get nervous because the old, compositor-run photosetting equipment was becoming unreliable and needed to be replaced. No one wanted to buy the old-style equipment, even if it was available, yet the print unions were still strong enough at this stage to deter managements from introducing the new direct input technology by force.

The NGA wanted its members to retain their jobs. Since money could only be saved by stopping double keying, managements did not want to introduce the new technology and keep all the printers and all the journalists in work. The National Union of Journalists (NUJ) saw the NGA's position as an attempt to turn printers into journalists and so put NUJ members' jobs at risk. In the end, both the NGA and the NUJ refused to work with the new equipment until it was decided who did what.

The *Portsmouth News* group tried to introduce the new technology against the wishes of the NUJ sparking a strike with NGA members setting the paper, many of them working as sub editors alongside Institute of Journalists' reporters and subs. At the *Wolverhampton Express and Star* the NGA was locked out for refusing to work the new system and NUJ members produced the papers using the new machines.

In 1986, the two unions forged an agreement on the introduction of new technology which spelt out who did what, and arranged for the retraining of NGA staff who would be redeployed. They also worked out details of the negotiations that would take place with provincial managements.

Within six months of the deal, more than twenty-five provincial newspapers, many of them dailies and many of them publishing a number of papers had reached agreement with the unions and introduced direct input.

Within two years there were very few papers national or provincial that were not printing using direct input and you would now be very hard pressed to find a paper in this country which does not print on direct input web-offset lithography.

Because of the late switch to this new technology, many papers went directly to full page make-up on screen. Most newspapers now use full-page make-up systems with journalists writing and designing on screen and the finished result being output as a plate ready to go straight onto the press.

Photographers have also joined the digital revolution with new cameras allowing images to be sent down phone lines and edited directly on computer. Direct input has also allowed a good deal more flexibility in the siting of presses. Telephone links allow direct input information to be sent from anywhere to anywhere allowing presses to be remote from the newsdesk. Journalists can now work in the centre of London or anywhere else and send the finished page electronically to a press situated outside London where it is cheaper but also more convenient for transport. Pages can also be sent to a multitude of sites allowing simultaneous printing in say London, Manchester, Bristol, Glasgow and Belfast easing distribution and transport costs and difficulties.

Letterpress

Letterpress is the process of impressing an inked relief surface against paper. The type and any artwork in this relief process are usually made of metal, etched to stand proud from the bed of the forme (the metal 'page'). It is set in mirror fashion so that its impression will appear the correct way round after imprinting.

Although letterpress is no longer as popular as it once was, particularly in periodicals, it is still one of the best and most efficient ways of printing small runs, cards and certain specialist non-colour runs. It provides a clear, crisp impression capable of extreme fidelity and consistency over long runs. It is not really capable of full colour, although it can produce spot colour and of course the ink used can be any colour the printer wants.

The basic press for relief printing is the platen machine. In this machine the type is held in a *chase* (a rectangular metal frame) to make a flat forme which is brought against the *platen* (a metal plate) with the paper in between, in a more or less vertical position. Rollers spread ink over the type immediately before printing. These machines range from small hand-operated machines for proofing and specialist applications, to larger power-operated machines. They are all sheet fed, although this can be done either by hand or automatically. All operate only mono colour although this can be anything from black to fluorescent pink or a metallic finish.

Cylinder machines

Platen machines would have been recognisable to the inventors of print. They would have found cylinder machines, sometimes called flatbed machines, less obvious.

In these machines, the forme still holds the flat relief printing surface but now this slides underneath a rotating cylinder which carries the sheet of paper into the press. These are capable of handling very large formes ($66'' \times 46''$), often with a number of pages which will later be guillotined to separate them.

Perfectors

Perfector machines use an elaboration of this principle to print on both sides. A cunning mechanical device grabs the sheet of paper coming of the plate cylinder and flips it so the other side of the paper hits the second plate cylinder. Some machines have several units to allow additional colours to be added to build up two, three or four colour images while some allow the perfector to be turned off so that the second cylinder can be used to add an extra colour while printing on one side only.

Rotary machines

Rotary machines print from curved plates or stereos. In all the previous machines, the type was held in a chase to make a flat relief surface know as a forme. Now an impression is taken of that forme known as a *flong*. This was originally made from papier mâché but on later machines, plastics were used. A process, patented first in the early nineteenth century, allowed this flong to be curved. A cast is made from this curved flong and this is loaded onto the printing cylinder of the rotary machine. Several pages will be loaded alongside each other and printed simultaneously. The paper is normally fed from a web between the impression cylinder and the plate cylinder, although there are some sheet-fed rotary presses. Curving the forme obviously distorts the print slightly and specialist types where developed to cope with this. The rotary's big advantage is high speed.

Modern developments have improved the method using plastic or rubber plates and even more recently photopolymer plates allowing full advantage to be taken of modern photo reproduction in both plate making and composition.

Lithography

Lithography has now overtaken letterpress as the main method of printing newspapers and magazines. It is probably possible to find a small weekly paper somewhere in the UK or US still using letterpress, but there can't be many. Most have either re-equipped, or have scrapped their expensive presses and sub-contracted the printing to one of the large presses now available. Few weekly papers print more that 50,000 copies and modern web-offset lithography presses can print that in under an hour.

The introduction of lithography was slow at first when the high cost of re-equipping could not be seen to be justified and although its principles were first espoused in 1798 by Aloys Senefelder and it flourished fairly quickly, it was not until the 1960s and 1970s that it became the dominant printing method in newspapers and magazines.

Lithography works on the principle that water and oil repel each other. A smoothed stone can be drawn on with a greasy crayon. If the stone is then wetted, the crayon will repel the water but the stone will remain wet. If the stone is then inked with a grease based ink, the ink will adhere only to the area touched by the crayon. The ink can then be transferred to the paper by direct contact. This method was of most use for images such as pictures and graphics that, until its invention, had been very difficult to produce with relief printing methods. However the process did not really take off for newspapers until it became *offset*. Offset printing means that the image is taken from the plate onto a flexible rubbery surface known as a blanket and it is this that prints onto the paper.

Stones are no longer used. Now a thin plate of aluminium is coated with a light-sensitive chemical. This allows the image to be transferred photographically to the plate either by photographing an image of the page onto the plate or, more likely these days, by direct output from a plate-making machine connected to the computer setting system. This plate is then treated so that the area to print will repel water and take up the ink. It is this direct link between photo-composition and the offset plate that has made offset printing so popular. Offset lithography is also popular because it makes it possible to produce full colour output. However, although it is a much more sophisticated process than letterpress it is nowhere near as robust. Because of the intense compression of the letterpress process, variations in paper, ink and plates were ironed out – literally.

In the offset process very careful balances have to be made between the amount of water (damping) and the amount of ink. This can be upset by even a small increase in humidity or temperature. All the contact surfaces involved in the process are also critical. As the system is a transfer of image rather than an impression as with letterpress, a slight variation can have disastrous effects.

Offset presses for newspapers are also a rotary process. The thin flexible aluminium plates are fixed around a cylinder and the paper is passed from a web between the blanket roller and the impression cylinder to pick up the image. Offset plates are thin and flexible and are easily wrapped around a cylinder without any noticeable distortion.

Some of the disadvantages of offset have been overcome by computer setting. Corrections used to be more difficult to make and plates were easily damaged. But now new plates can be made from a corrected computer photo image within minutes if not seconds. The advantages of using colour, and high quality photo images make offset ideal for printing newspapers and magazines.

To colour print requires passing the paper through four different impressions, one for each of the colours used in the process including black. Because each colour must print accurately over the others to produce a true colour image, the plates must be carefully aligned if registration is to be achieved. Difficult though this process is, the technique was impossible for relief printing because of the stresses set up by the process. The more subtle offset litho, however, allows good quality images to be made in full colour.

With the high speeds used by modern web-offset machines, a number of problems come up of which journalists need to be aware. The technical difficulties of balancing ink and water mean that web-offset is very wasteful of paper with up to 12 per cent wasted running a press up to its full speed. A paper break means rethreading and rerunning-up – a massive loss in time and in paper.

Presses are also inflexible with regard to the size of the final job. The size of the cylinder and the positioning of the folder cutter and other end of press features mean that most presses are designed to print only one length or 'cut off' giving any particular press fixed dimensions for its publications so that it is only able to print a broadsheet or tabloid to those dimensions.

Gravure

Gravure is the giant of printing. It is a complex process ideal for colour work that gives high quality, consistent results but which is suitable only for extremely long runs.

Gravure is an intaglio process – the reverse of relief. The print cylinders are engraved directly with the areas that are not to be printed, being etched away. The etched sections hold the ink that is then transferred to the paper.

The depth of etching can be varied and this is the clever bit. A very shallow pit will hold less ink and therefore produce a lighter tonal value than a deep pit. In this way, gradations of tone can be added. Both offset and letterpress put a consistent level of ink on the paper and are able to vary density of colour only by screening to build up a series of different sized dots that will give the impression of tonal gradation. The surface of the gravure plate is engraved in a series of cells with a depth varying from 25/1,000 of a millimetre to 1/5,000 of a millimetre. The gaps between the cells is very small and although when in action the printing cylinder is wiped clear of ink by a blade called the doctor blade these microscopic lips have of necessity been inked slightly. This helps join up the gap between the cells giving the impression of continuity.

Stamps are an excellent example of the quality of work that can be accomplished with gravure. Gravure is also used for things like packaging and can print on paper, card and film.

Composition

Composition is no longer the skilled process that it used to be. Most newspapers and magazines are produced using computer systems that allow journalists to write their stories are one end of the process, for sub-editors to edit and design the material and for finished plates to come out at the other end. There are very few places left where the composing room puts together the pages.

Web feed

As much of the cost of offset is in paper and offset is very wasteful on run-up, good feed systems and automatic reel changeover is vital. This is particularly important considering that a big press producing a 32-page paper requires at least four separate reels all inevitably running out at different times.

Presses are load with two reels that run through a tensioner. As the paper is close to running out, the paper feed is laid close to a new reel, the end of which is coated with sticky tape. As the reel is close to ending, the paper feed is pressed against the tape, picking up the feed from the new reel, at the same time the old paper feed is sliced. The tensioner ensures that variations in the feed during this process are ironed out. The newspapers with the stuck together bits of paper are later jettisoned by a machine minder.

Post press

After the paper is printed, it has to be collated, cut and folded. Several sheets are often split and always collated so that all the webs come together in the correct order. They are drawn together folded and then cut. In broadsheet papers they would be folded again. They are then stacked, bundled and bound together.

Photo reproduction

Because letterpress and offset litho are both continuous processes, they do not allow directly for tonal gradations, they can only print in 100 per cent ink density or zero ink density. Pictures and tones, therefore, can only be printed as *halftones*. The image will appear either in the ink colour or the paper colour. This will generally be black or white.

In order to represent the continuous range of tones in a photograph or to add shading and tonal variety, the picture is broken down into a series of dots. The larger the dot, the darker the tone will appear.

Traditionally, a photograph is re-photographed through a cross-line screen (usually as any reduction or enlargement required is made). The screen is made up from two sheets of glass. Each sheet is engraved with a series of parallel lines. These lines are etched out with hydrofluoric acid and filled with an opaque pigment. The width of the transparent lines separating the opaque lines is the same as the width of the opaque lines. Two such sheets are stuck together so that the lines are at right angles to form a grid where the transparent area is now only 25 per cent of the screen. The screen is placed between the lens of the camera and the photographic emulsion. Each transparent area now acts as a pin-hole camera on the very small area of image acting upon it and producing an image in which the size of the image is relative to the brightness; the brighter the image, the smaller the dot. In this way the image is broken up into a series of dots of equal density and gradient but of different sizes.

Nowadays, most photographs are scanned into the computer system or are imported directly from the photographer's digital camera. The computer sets up the screening process after the picture has been edited and placed on a page. Screening is then automatically applied to the photograph before the plate is printed. However, it is worth remembering the traditional screen with its opaque lines because this can make it easier to understand the terminology. Photographs can be screened with a different number of lines per linear centimetre (the raster). Different densities of lines allow for different effects. A 26-line screen (26 lines to the linear centimetre) is coarse and gives low-grade results suitable only for the poor quality of paper used in newspapers. A 60-line per linear centimetre screen would produce good results on coated stock while the finest detailed work might require 150 lines per linear centimetre (Durrant 1989: 55). A daily newspaper typically uses a raster of 31.5 lines per linear cm or 80 lines per inch (80 lpi) (Kammermeier and Kammermeier 1992: 69). Sometimes the lines are measured in inches and a screen will be expressed as 75 lines per inch (lpi). This is becoming more common because although Britain has been moving towards metric measurements, many of our computer based printing machines are US-made, where imperial measurements are still the norm.

The angle at which the raster lines are presented is also important. The screen is normally put at 45° to the perpendicular for mono work. In two-colour work the main colour will be at 45° while the lighter colour will be at 75°. In four-colour work black will be at 45°, magenta at 15°, cyan at 75° and yellow at 90° (ibid.).

Output

The main decision to be made when outputting an edited photograph to a plate maker or image setter is the *raster dot* resolution. Once the picture has been edited, cropped, sized etc., we will need to output it. In order to output a black and white halftone from the computer, either separately or as part of a page we need to convert the intermediate greys into patterns of dots as we did with the process camera. However, the image setter can only produce one size of dot. Since the number of halftones capable of being reproduced depends on the number of dots per inch the output device is capable of delivering, provided sufficient information is scanned in, the computer clumps together a number of these dots available in its output to form the screen patterns. Thus an image setter outputting at 1,200 dots per inch on a halftone whose screen has been set to 200 lines per inch will be using a block of 6×6 dots to make up each raster dot. However, this cell size will give a maximum of only 36 grey scales. Since the human eye can see at least 64 shades, and can certainly tell the difference between a 64-shade and a 256-shade halftone, we would normally want to increase the number of shades from 36 to anything from the acceptable 64 shades up to a perfect 256 shades. This would require a bigger cell of output dots to allow more variation in the raster dot. We can calculate the number of dots in the screen cell by dividing the image setter resolution in lines per inch by the raster. If the setter can reproduce 2,400 dots per inch and we want a raster of

120, then we have a grid of 10×10 dots to make our output raster dot giving us 100 shades of grey, not perfect, but certainly giving a reasonable image. A 4,800 dots per inch image setter would allow a grid of 20×20 or 400 grey scales. This is more than enough and would allow the potential for a 16×16 grid to give 256 shades and up to 150 raster lines.

Since the number of dots in the cell directly relates to the number of grey scales, we can use this to calculate the best screen setting by squaring the number of dots in the raster cell (Kammermeier and Kammermeier 1992: 72)

Screen cell	Grey scale
4×4	16
6×6	36
8×8	64
16×16	256

We can calculate the number of grey shades by dividing the square of the printed dots per inch (the maximum output of the printer) by the square of the raster.

This means the number of grey scales $= \left(\dfrac{dpi}{raster}\right)^2$. If you were to possess a printer capable of 2,400 dots per inch and you screened at 120 lines per inch then the number of halftones would be: $\left(\dfrac{2,400}{120}\right)^2 = 400$. Since it is extremely unlikely that we would have scanned in more than 256 grey scales, this information is not likely to be available to print out. This means that we could instead have a smaller raster dot and more lines per inch.

The quality of the paper is also important. Newsprint for instance, cannot handle a line image of 120. The ink soaks into the paper and spreads making dots finer than 100 lines per inch pointless. Most newsprint screens are in the region 70–90. Colour might use a finer screen. When it comes to producing colour, then four outputs are required to represent full colour – each output is produced as described above.

The calculations above will help us determine the resolution required to output the image.

Scanners

In order to output a photograph, we need to input it into the computer first. This can be done either by importing a digital photograph directly from the camera or by scanning the photograph. Direct input is becoming more common with staff photographers and freelances using digital cameras as standard. However, a picture will often come from an outside source as a print and this will need to be scanned in.

In computing terms full colour is represented by the three primary colours. Each can have up to 256 tonal variations (the eye cannot detect more than 256 different shades). This gives a total of 16.7 million colours ($256 \times 256 \times 256$). Each of the 256 tonal variations of a primary colour can be represented by an 8-bit number. All 16.7 million colours therefore require a 24-bit number. Hence the expression 24-bit colour. Modern colour scanners work at up to 48-bit depth. These allow for a greater number of shades to be scanned in. This is because the photograph will be darkened in the printing process. By making the picture lighter for publication, many of the very light shades of grey will be removed and the darker greys are enhanced. If there are far more grey shades (up to 4,096 shades in a 36-bit scanner) then there are more dark greys to work with and the picture can still be 256 shades once the picture has been published.

When we come to input a picture into the computer (from whatever source) we need to decide on the resolution. The higher the resolution, the better the potential quality when outputting. However, scanning is very different from outputting. Scanners look at a very small area of the picture and render it as a dot (a pixel) by measuring the shade of the picture either in colour or black and white, depending on which you have asked for. The user can adjust the size of the area measured up to 2,400 dots per inch. These scanned dots relate directly to the pixels on the computer screen. The modern PC screen set at XGA mode can display 800×600 pixels. Some larger screens can show resolutions up to $1,600 \times 1,400$ pixels. A picture scanned at 800×600 pixels will fill the Extended Graphical Array (XGA) screen whatever size it really is. In other words, if you instruct the scanner to scan at 100 dots per inch, then an eight-inch picture will be 800 dots wide and so will fill the screen. But a two-inch picture scanned at a resolution of 400 dots per inch, will also fill the screen. The result will depend on the software of course and a picture loaded into a desktop publishing package will appear in the size you have asked for because the software will copy the picture at the correct resolution for standard output at the size you have requested. The dots relate directly to the raster dot to be output by the image setter. Each raster dot output is intended to represent a shade of grey (for grey-scale pictures) or the shades of the four output colours for colour work.

When scanning in a picture, the temptation is to go for a very high resolution on the assumption that this will give the best results, but this is not necessarily true. If, for instance, you are scanning a black and white picture for a newspaper with a raster of 80 lines per inch, then your maximum output will be 80 lines per inch (80 lpi). In other words, your output device will be trying to represent one out of 256 different shades of grey per 1/80 inch. But your scanner can represent 256 different shades of grey as a colour. It will only convert it to a half-screen dot when it is output. Thus, provided you don't want to enlarge the picture on outputting, you can scan at a resolution of 80 dots per inch, as these will be capable of representing one of the 256 shades of grey every eightieth of an inch. There is no point in giving a higher resolution, because that is the resolution you are going to print at. The only reason for a higher scanning resolution is if you intend to enlarge the picture. Assuming you knew you wanted to make the picture twice as large, then you should scan it in at 160 dots per inch (160 dpi), so that when you output at twice the size, you will be able to do so with a raster of (80 lpi).

We should remember that as we adjust the size of our picture in the computer, the amount of information scanned in remains constant. The computer merely juggles the information to give the impression of size change. A picture scanned at 100 dots dpi and then reduced to 25 per cent of its original size, now has only 25 pixels representing an inch on the screen, but it is in fact 400 dpi. Similarly, if the picture were increased to 400 per cent it would have only 25 dpi and the pixels would appear to be four times as big. When pictures are enlarged, the pixels can often become so big, that the picture appears to be made up of a number of square shapes. If the computer did not juggle the information received, then we would not be able to alter the picture later. If you have ever reduced the size of an image in Photoshop, saved the result and then tried to re-enlarge it to its original size, you will have seen that the computer struggled to enlarge it because the extra information needed to enlarge the picture had been ditched.

There is also the problem of file size. The higher the scan resolution, the larger the file: the processing time will be longer and the computer system is more likely to fail in attempts to print.

The following chart shows approximate file sizes for an 8 in × 6 in 256-grey scale picture (8-bit).

Scan res (dpi)	File size
100	480K
200	2Mb
400	8Mb
800	31Mb

You will notice that as the scan resolution is doubled, the file size is quadrupled. This is because the scan resolution is only linear while the file size represents area.

Since the only consequence of scanning at too high a resolution is to make for very large files with consequent storage problems, it is best to scan the picture at the right size to start with. If you know by how much you need the picture enlarged then this should be taken into account, but assuming the picture will be used at about the same size or smaller, the scan resolution should be 1.4 times the raster dot size:

Scan resolution = raster resolution × 1.4

If the picture is to be substantially altered, then the following equation can be used:

$$\text{Scan resolution} = \text{raster resolution} \times 1.4 \times \frac{\text{desired size}}{\text{original size}}$$ (Kammermeier and Kammermeier 1992: 83)

COLOUR PRINT PROCESS

So far I have talked largely about grey scale – black and white printing. But much work nowadays, especially in magazines, is in colour. Some newspapers still use spot colour printing. This is where the work is printed in one colour – usually black on white paper, and then another colour is printed on top of that. The second colour is known as a spot colour. It allows for emphasis on mastheads, advertiser titles and elsewhere. It was widely used on letterpress as a way of adding emphasis.

In spot colour the inks can be of any colour you like. The hue, saturation and value can all be adjusted by the printer using a different colour of ink in the same way that you can buy different shades of paint from a DIY store.

However with spot colour, once that colour is chosen for a page or block of pages, you are stuck with it and it must be used for the whole page. Hence spot colours in newspapers tend to be easy primaries. This is particularly true of contract printers who may not be keen to clean out the spot colour unit to change from their usual red to orange just for you.

The tabloid nationals are often called red tops by virtue of the spot colour they use. Now that most presses are capable of producing full colour, spot colour is not so widely used. The other problem with spot colour is the impossibility of getting accurate register. In spot colour the press prints one colour and then the other. The process of registration – ensuring that the two colours are overlaid exactly in the same place – is difficult and expensive. Spot colour can only really be used on areas where it doesn't matter if the colours slip slightly.

Process colour

Process colour is more flexible although more expensive. Full colour allows the reproduction of all shades of colour.

Our eyes see the primary colours of red, green and blue and TV sets use light guns of these colours to make up the range of realistic colours we see on our screens. A lot of red and a little green and no blue gives you a vivid red/orange. But if you tried this with coloured pens on a piece of paper, all you would get is a nasty muddy brown. Printing uses a subtractive method – the complete opposite of the additive method outlined above. It uses the secondary colours to make up the colours we eventually see. Secondary colours are the complementary colours to the three primary colours. The complementary to green is magenta, the complementary to blue is yellow and the complementary to red is cyan.

When all these secondary colours are present, they print black, when all are absent they print white (provided you are using white paper). Add yellow and blue together and you will get the primary colour green.

For printing, the secondary colours of cyan, magenta and yellow are usually combined with black. This is because of deficiencies in ink. Although theoretically, combining the secondaries should give black, in fact the best possible outcome is a muddy brown. The addition of black ink allows the printer to produce pure black and to alter the value of the colours from full black to white. Black is represented by the letter K to give the CMYK system.

The colours are separated out in the computer to produce four separations. These are used to make four different plates. The plates are loaded onto the press and print one on top of the other to produce a colour reproduction. The black plate also carries the type, rather than have that reproduced on four plates. Each plate is printed in register. That is, they print precisely on top of each other. If they miss by even a small amount, the picture will look blurry and odd. A slight cast of one colour will appear around the left hand outline of everything and a cast of another colour around the right hand outline. Massive improvements have been made in colour reproduction over the past few years as presses become more capable and as equipment improves. The poor quality of colour images common twenty years ago is now rare.

If you want a tone patch of a certain colour, you can mark the page with the percentages of each colour or the pantone number and the printer will arrange for the colour separation to include the information.

Pantone is a system for identifying shades of colour that gives every shade a number. Editors can choose a shade from a book and give the printer the code. Pantone colour 150U for instance would be mixed with 0 per cent cyan, 31 per cent magenta, 60 per cent yellow and 0 per cent black to give a light orange. The editor could also simply give the colour percentages, but unless the editor has a book with the shades in it, that might not mean very much. In this way the saturation and lightness of each colour can be adjusted and this varies how they will mix to provide the final shades.

5
Pre-planning and copy tasting

Producing a new *edition* of any publication requires you to go through a number of planning stages. These usually start with the advertising. Advertising is a key ingredient of any publication produced in the western, capitalist tradition. Whether we journalists like it or not, it is advertising that generally pays the bills and makes a profit allowing the company to continue in business. There are a few publications that can exist on subscription and sales income alone, but these tend to be very expensive and very specialist. The mainstream publications rely on advertising for a large part of their income.

Because of the importance of advertising space, the first thing to do when planning an edition is to see how many adverts there are and where they will be placed as this will influence the size of the publication and determine what you can put on each page.

Someone in the advertising sales department will normally be responsible for planning the placement of advertising. They will normally discuss a draft with the editor or production editor. Some adjustments might be made because there are too many ads on one page, or because a special feature is going on certain pages and room needs to be made or particular advertisers excluded. Sometimes the advertising department will ask for specific advertisers to go on a particular page alongside certain stories or features and this might pose an ethical dilemma for the editor. It might be fine for a TV rental firm or video hire shop to advertise on the TV listings page of a newspaper, but it would be less acceptable to allow an advert from a local company to sit on the page containing a story about their winning a queen's award to industry. After the discussion the editor will be left with a firm decision of how many pages the *edition* will include and what space will be available to the editorial department on each page.

DECIDING ON COPY ALLOCATION

Once an edition has been agreed upon, the editor will want to draw up a page plan that allows him or her to decide what will go on each page and determine the structure of the edition. A lot of these decisions might be standardised – sports section at the back, for instance – but the editor will still need to consider things. During the World Cup or Olympic Games, for instance, a newspaper might decide to move sport to the front rather than run it at the back; a fairly radical move, but one that should be considered. There's nothing worse than doing something just because that's how you've always done it. On the other hand, there's no point in changing something for the sake of it. Readers come to expect certain things in certain places and get cross if they can't find them. Many newspapers now put the TV listings in the centre of the paper to make it easy for people to find them; magazines have index pages at the front and regular spots (such as agony aunts or the stars) in regular spaces, often at the back.

The page plan can be made on the computer or on paper. Newspapers have traditionally used dummies – mock-ups of the newspaper produced by folding A4 sheets of paper to represent the paper (see Figure 5.1). A listing is also helpful and can be used alongside a dummy as a quick reminder of what is where in that edition of the newspaper (see Figure 5.2). This doesn't work as well for large newspapers or magazines and might be better accomplished with a flat plan (see Figure 5.3).

A listing is useful for seeing how the edition will look overall. A flat plan or *dummy* allows allocation of space for adverts and editorial material on specific pages. Producing plans in hard copy rather than on the computer allows the editor to take them to planning meetings and editorial conferences. They can also be used in discussion with designers, subs and other staff.

Selecting pages

The editor will decide what goes where on the basis of need and tradition. Nowadays news goes on the front and first few inside pages of a newspaper or on the first few inside pages of a magazine. Tabloid papers may well have far more of the inside pages covered with news than broadsheets and might feel the need to break these up with specialist pages more often than a broadsheet in order to offer some variety.

Left v. right pages

One of the big debates in newspaper and to a lesser extent, magazine design is the left page versus right page dilemma. Some editors believe that the reader

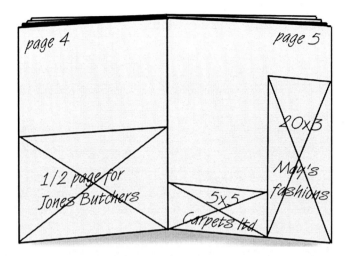

Figure 5.1 A *dummy* shows where the adverts go in a mock-up of the publication

23/10/06	Nevermore Gazette		
1	News	36	Sport
2	International news	35	Sport
3	News	34	Sport
4	Weddings	33	Sport
5	News	32	classified
6	News	31	classified
7	News	30	classified
8	Full page ad	29	classified
9	News	28	classified
10	Readers' letters	27	classified
11	Full page ad	26	classified
12	Features	25	classified
13	Features – fashion	24	classified
14	Features - fashion	23	classified
15	Entertainment	22	Wedding pics
16	Entertainment/what's on	21	Ad feature
17	Travel/leisure	20	Personal finance
18	TV listings	19	TV listings

Figure 5.2 A contents listing. A quick guide to what is where. Also shows which pages will be alongside each other on the press. For instance, pages 1 and 36 will print together, as will pages 18 and 19. If they are printed by a colour unit, they will all have colour

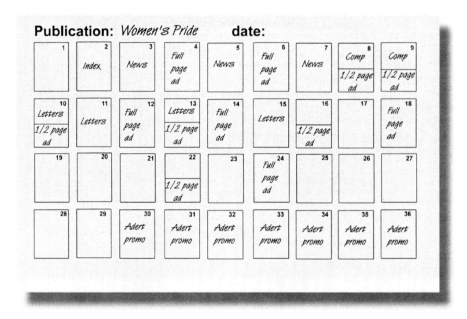

Figure 5.3 A flat plan. Useful for large publications as it allows you to see all the pages at once

will tend to look at the right-hand page first because as they open the paper, this will be the first page they see. This is somewhat debatable for one or two reasons. Readers are trained by practice to look at the top left-hand corner of any reading matter as this is where we are used to starting with books. You don't open a book and look automatically at the right-hand page, you tend to look at the left hand page. The Poynter Institute's Eye-trac research (Garcia and Stark 1991) shows that readers look at facing pages as a whole and do not distinguish between them. On the other hand, Garcia also points out that large picture or display areas on a page will draw the reader and inevitably they will see the right-hand page first and any graphic, picture or display area it contains. They might, therefore, be attracted to reading this first.

Krees and Van Leeuwen (1996: 186) believe that the right and left pages of magazines have a particular information value. They call this 'the given' and 'the new'. The right-hand page offers new information, key to the story while the left hand page gives what is already known. They see the left leading into the right: moving from the given to the new.

> Looking at what is placed on the left and what is placed on the right in other kinds of visuals confirms this generalization: when pictures or layouts make significant use of the horizontal axis, positioning some of their elements left,

and other, different ones right of the centre (which does not, of course, happen in every composition) the elements placed on the left are presented as Given, the elements placed on the right as New.

(Krees and Van Leeuwen 1996: 186)

Krees and Van Leeuwen do not however suggest this applies to newspapers, only to magazines where the material is placed on two pages straddling the horizontal axis.

Whatever the actual readership habits, editors, by and large, still believe that the right-hand pages (odd numbered pages) are of more importance. For this reason, adverts are kept off the first few right-hand pages if possible. Almost always, the first full page advert you will find in a newspaper will be on a left-hand page, in an attempt to give editorial dominance. You will rarely find adverts that fill both facing pages, although this has more to do with the advertiser's need to keep the reader reading editorial material alongside an advert.

Adverts are also kept to a minimum on right-hand pages for the same reason. It may well be the case (with the large page size of the average newspaper) that as the reader turns the page, if the first thing they saw was an advert, they might well continue until they found editorial matter. But if Garcia's argument is true then readers deal with left and right pages as a whole and might be attracted anywhere on those two pages. They certainly do not treat the left and right page as separate entities to be read differently (Garcia and Stark 1991). It is important to remember that it might be better to plan and design the pages as an entity rather than deal with them separately. You will see in the plan above (Figures 5.1 and 5.2), that it follows a traditional viewpoint, putting pages such as readers' letters and weddings on the left-hand pages opposite news pages. It is assumed in the traditional view that regular features that have a strong reader interest such as letters, weddings, stars and agony aunts can be placed anywhere and that readers will seek them out. News on the other hand needs to attract a fickle reader and draw them in and requires all the assistance that editorial expertise can give.

Spreads

Spreads allow a designer to go to town on an idea. A *spread* is the use of facing pages to work on a single feature or news item tying the left and right page together. It needs to be remembered when working for newspapers that the technology of the press means that there will be a gutter (margins) between the two pages and that this can make it difficult to join the two together. Headlines and pictures cannot easily be run over the two pages as there will be a 3–4 cm gap between the two pages. The exception to this is the centre spread.

The centre pages are printed as one piece on the press. The average press, whether printing tabloid or broadsheet, prints several pages on the same piece of paper and then splits them before gathering the pages together and folding them into a newspaper. This means that many pages are printed alongside each other and could technically be bled together. Looking at the page listing (Figure 5.2 above) shows us which pages are printed together. The front and back for instance are printed alongside each other. Indeed, on most presses for a tabloid paper, the front, back and two centre pages are printed alongside each other with the inside front, inside back, inside centres printed on the opposite side. The front and back are then cut off and the pages gathered and folded to make a newspaper.

This is important to understand because it allows us to decide on colour use. Most presses only have two or three colour units so that colour can only be printed on two or three blocks of pages that are printed together. So, for instance, the front, back and centre pages might be printed in colour, because they are printed alongside each other, but the inside back and front might not, because they do not have a colour unit. The publication listing above helps us to decide which pages have colour because we know that pages listed opposite each other will be printed together and so will have colour if colour is available on that unit.

This is important because it allows us to decide which pages should go where. For instance, readers' letters probably do not need colour, while the wedding pictures page might well look better with colour. We would ensure that letters go on a page without colour while wedding pictures go on a page with colour.

The front and back of a newspaper normally have colour, which means the inside centre also has colour. The inside centre pages are printed together, so these are the only pages that do not have a margin. This means that we can print across the two pages without a gutter. Headlines, graphics and photographs can span the two without problems. For this reason, many editors don't like putting TV listings or adverts in the centre, they'd rather use the space for a more interesting and expansive feature or news story. Fashion is often placed across this centre spread as it allows more attractive designs and colour than is possible elsewhere in a newspaper. This helps explain the enthusiasm for 'supplements'. Newspapers will often have a TV or entertainment supplement inserted in the newspaper. By this method, the editor can use a two-page spread, but deeper in the paper. By persuading the reader that they should remove the 4- or 8- (or even 12- or 16-) page supplement, there is then an additional two-page spread on what is in reality two inside pages.

Of course none of this is a problem in a magazine; colour is available on all pages, and there is no gutter to worry about because pages are bled to the edge. However, it is still not always easy to spread across two pages and full page adverts are more prevalent as the pages are smaller than a newspaper. In advertising, although having what advertisers call *solus* position (the only ad on a page) is important, so is the actual size. Having a half page ad in an A4 magazine means a smaller ad than half page in a tabloid. Therefore big advertisers will normally seek a full page advert in a magazine and they would prefer this to be facing editorial material so that the reader will pause to read and therefore (the theory goes) read the ad. For this reason, it is more usual to have only one page in a magazine.

What should go where?

General decisions about where in the publication things should go will depend on the publication, its style, content and readership. Most newspapers and magazines prefer to have news near the start of the publication. Newspapers have news from the front page on. There is no particular reason for this other than tradition. Many newspapers used to carry nothing but adverts on the front page, some until relatively recently.

Because the first few pages carry the latest news, their deadlines are normally as late as possible. This ensures that news pages are the last to be finished, so that the news is the freshest part of the publication. Deadlines are set to allow the flow of copy and the production of the paper to follow an orderly pattern. Some pages have to be designed and produced first and it makes sense for these to be feature pages that can be prepared well in advance leaving the news pages to be produced last.

In a typical evening paper, the features and entertainments pages are normally produced the afternoon before. Many of the news pages will also be *overnights*: pages produced well before the final deadline. Often only the front and back page and possibly one or two specially dedicated *live pages* will be left to be filled the following morning with stories gathered in the past evening or morning of publication. Right-hand pages feature strongly in these live pages and it is likely to be pages three and five that are the last to be designed before page one.

Copy tasting

Once the various pages have been agreed upon, the editor, production editor or chief sub has to decide how the copy is allocated to the pages. In larger offices, the pages might be divided up so that all the features pages are allocated to the features editor, sports pages to the sports editor and news pages to the chief sub-editor. On a really big newspaper even the news pages might be split between the foreign, home and other news desks.

Copy is then *tasted* – looked at to decide how and where the copy should be used. All the stories or features that are available will be considered by the appropriate editor and a decision made about where to use it and in what form.

When it comes to news, this is quite a complex process. A really good story might be difficult to use because there is so little information; and while it might be entirely newsworthy, it might be difficult to fit such a small amount of copy onto the page and give it a suitable display. Another story might be tedious, but require a considerable amount of material to make it worth using. An example of the first scenario could be that the police announce they have arrested the prime minister for treason. A big story no doubt, that requires us to use it on the front page of a newspaper. But the law prevents newspapers from reporting much detail following the arrest of someone for a crime and, legally at least, there is little that the newspaper can report. The page might end up being a huge picture of the prime minister, enormous headlines and 150 words of copy.

On the anniversary of the September 11 terrorist attacks however, every newspaper felt obliged to run copy on the first few pages, including the front, yet little of this was new or unexpected. There was a lot of material, but finding something dramatic or new was very difficult.

It could also be that there are six good stories that could all be used on the front page, but all have at least two good pictures and eight hundred words of copy. There would not be enough room to fit this news feast on the front page. Discussions then have to take place about which stories are moved inside. Copy tasting is about selecting the right stories to run and then putting them on the right page with other stories to make balanced and interesting pages that the reader will enjoy reading.

Copy style

When the paper or magazine is first designed, the designer will decide not just about fonts and artwork, but also have some ideas of how different pages will look. This could be fixed by producing a series of templates that can be used for different pages. I discuss templates in more depth in Chapter 7, but essentially templates are ways of producing page layouts that can be lifted into the computer from central storage allowing the sub to fill in the spaces; a headline here of a certain size, some copy there and a picture over here. It removes the need for detailed design skills but it can also lead to very samey looking pages. Even if templates are not used, the designer will still want to lay down a house style – rules about the way pages should look. This might have rules such as: no more than two lines of heading if the lead heading is across more than four columns, no reverse headings above the fold (the half-way point on a newspaper where it is folded, usually only applies to the front page as people can only read the inside if it is unfolded). Pictures should always be above or below the fold, never across it. The style might be very detailed giving little latitude for *byline* styles, intros, captions, caption placement, picture styles, whether you can *pierce* pictures and so on. This style needs to be followed as far as possible.

6
Designing pages

Once copy has been allocated to a page, someone is going to have to design it; to decide on the amount and type of display and how the page will be structured. Many of these decisions are taken by the editor, production editor or chief sub-editor. These executives will have already discussed in conference which of the stories will lead the page and approximately how it should be handled – a major splash treatment for an important story or just tucked down the middle of the page with something above it if it is not so significant? These decisions are important because even at this display level we need to be truthful with the readers. Giving a weak story major splash treatment is to oversell it. The reader is likely to end up confused – the display suggested the story was important and it turns out that it wasn't. There is an area of science called false alarm theory that shows that constant false alarms reduce a person's trust in an alarm system. There is no reason to suppose this does not apply to newspapers and magazines as well, and so if we keep saying that something is a great story and it turns out not to be, the reader will end up not trusting the paper and will therefore probably take another. So what could we do instead? Well, we could offer them value for money. Give plenty of stories and pictures on that page – all interesting but none of them heart-stopping. Many magazines do this with their news pages. None of the news is startling – it is all about an area of interest – new products, manufacturing changes, latest techniques or inventions, handy tips or gossip. All of it is of interest to the target group and a couple of busy pages filled with small items and pictures can give a lot of information and reader satisfaction.

The daily conference of newsroom executives may have decided the lead, and possibly the main picture story. Other stories on the page will be selected by the chief sub, probably in some sort of order. The chief sub will then brief the designer, explaining how the copy should be handled. The chief sub may well offer far more copy than can be fit on the page and so it is then up to the designer to decide on the amount of copy required and the amount of display material. Sub-editors can then be instructed about the length of copy required for each page.

THE TRADITIONAL METHOD

Although most newspapers and magazines are made up on computer desktop publishing systems such as Quark Xpress or Aldus Pagemaker it is still worth discussing the traditional method of designing pages. This is partly because there may still be some places that do not use computer systems and partly because the traditional ways often have something to teach us.

When pages were still made up by compositors, either in metal in the composing room or with photocomposition on light tables, journalists and designers had to produce a draft of the way the page should look. This had to be very detailed to ensure there could be no mistake about the design. It would show where the copy was to go, it would detail the headlines and give their sizes and it would mark up where the pictures should go and their sizes. Often this detailed draft would be preceded by a rough visualisation of the page, particularly if the page was complicated or was a busy feature page (news is often easier to design as there is just a series of news 'blocks' or 'modules' to be put together).

This page visualisation is extremely useful in helping to grasp scale and to provoke ideas. Original ideas in design, as in writing, are paramount. Original pages that work and stay in house style (approximately at least) are what set apart good publications from ordinary ones.

In my experience, beginners, whether students or practitioners, find the idea of a visual difficult. I always insist that students produce a visual first, but often they try to avoid this and go straight onto the computer. I am convinced that they are hoping that their nervousness at being faced by a pristine piece of paper which they have to turn into a page of a publication will vanish on the computer and that it will magically do the work for them. Certainly their first stumbling attempts do appear to look more professional on the computer – they're bound to! However, it can take them an hour to lay in their first couple of stories on the computer and then when they find the design doesn't work, they have to scrap it and start again. Producing a visual – once you have some experience – takes only a few moments. If the plan doesn't work, it can be thrown away and a new attempt made, building on what was learned from the failed attempt.

The visual can be produced on a piece of scrap paper (see Figure 6.1). This does not need to be very big and is only intended to work out the main elements of the page and give a rough idea of fit and scale. These visuals will not only help you to work out how it will fit but should spark off ideas that will make the page more attractive and interesting.

In the traditional office, the visual would have been replaced by an accurate representation of how the page should look when it is finished, but in a computerised office, this is not necessary and when you are happy with the general feel of the page, you can start laying out the frames on the page in the computer.

Whether you are doing a visual for a traditional office or a computerised office always check that you have the right adverts for the page, that they are the right size and that they have been drawn to the right size. There is nothing worse than drawing up a page and then finding that an ad marked as three columns was clearly marked 4×12. Once you are sure you have all the ads and any other items such as mastheads and blurbs in the right place you can start drawing – using pencil!

Figure 6.1 A visual: a quick sketch to try ideas, see how the page might look and get a sense of scale

The visual is there entirely to help you get clear in your mind how the page should look. Although any old scrap of paper can be used, it's probably better to use a piece of A4 so that it is similar in proportions to the page you will be designing. Using a piece of paper smaller than the final page means that you will be working on a scaled down version and this can be a bit confusing at first. The smaller size of the visual makes the page look different to the finished item. This is something you will need to get used to as you will often work on the page on computer at about this size. Very few screens are able to show you the whole of a tabloid page at full size. You must either see only a section of the page or switch to full page view which will reduce the scale of the page to as little as 25 per cent. However, if you find it very difficult to cope with the difference in scale, there is nothing to stop you using a piece of A3 paper, which will be very similar in size to tabloid.

Some places still use pre-printed pro-formas for visuals. These have grids on them to show the columns and scaled down depth in centimetres (see Figure 6.2). These grids can be particularly useful in your early days as you start to get the hang of scale on a visual (see Figure 6.1). You might want to photocopy the grid shown in Figure 6.2 to use for yourself when you practise producing visuals. It would be worth enlarging it when you photocopy. If you prefer, you can draw up your own using your DTP package.

Figure 6.2 A grid for a tabloid page (38 cm useable depth) and seven columns. Allows the designer to draft accurate pages

A page draft is different to a visual in that a draft should be an accurate representation of the page you are designing to enable someone else to make the page up. A draft is used when a compositor is producing the page either on computer or in traditional hot metal or photocomposition. It is unlikely that this will happen in many publications in the US or UK, but there are still plenty of places in the world using this tried and tested technology. Remember – if something can be read the wrong way on a draft it will be. Make sure you label everything clearly and accurately.

Figure 6.3 A page draft. Note that all the detail required is listed: headline and picture sizes and so on

It is important to produce a good quality draft (see Figure 6.3) in order to cut out mistakes and misinterpretations. The page should fit together accurately but this will not happen if your draft is sloppy. Make sure that you accurately measure the right space for pictures, graphics and headings. Headings are represented by a line running within the depth the heading will take. The heading size and style should be clearly written on the lines.

The actual heading can be added when the sub has written it. Non-standard measures and type sizes should be clearly marked. Single column runs can be marked by a single line, but jumps to another column should be clearly tracked. All captions, bylines and other type devices should be marked as well as rules and any other design elements.

The *catchline* of every piece of copy should be written within a circle over where it is to be placed. Pictures or any graphic are marked with crossed lines. At the centre a circle should be drawn to take the picture *catchline* and size. It is well worth writing the size and measure of any non-standard type on the page so that the *stone sub* can easily get it reset if it should go missing.

Remember: a draft must be accurate, and non-ambiguous. It has to be read against a deadline by someone who has no idea what you had in mind and maybe doesn't care.

Much of the same applies to a draft made on the computer. If you have a completely integrated system, the adverts will already be on the page (or at least the space for them). If the system does not automatically connect with advertising, then you will have to check again that you have planned in the right size adverts. You can then insert the frames according to the design in your visualisation, making detailed changes as necessary. You can also add additional material as needed. Once the frames are in place, the copy can be placed after subbing, the headlines written and the pictures edited. Once last-minute adjustments have been made and the page has been fully checked, it can be sent for plate-making.

FIRST STEPS

Just as the first few words of a story are the most agonising to come up with while you debate how best to sully the framed bright whiteness of the computer screen, so the first tentative lines of a design are usually the most stressful and difficult. It can help to run through your mind what type of stories you have to display on the page, their relative merits and any weighting the chief sub has asked you give them.

Write the stories down in a list and consider them. How much copy is there and what are your instructions about its use? Do they have any pictures to illustrate them? If so, are they any good? Could you find some more pictures?

Example 1: You have been given the following copy for a newspaper news page:

Story	Length	Instructions
Family home blaze – no deaths	26 cm	lead story with pix
Council to change planning system	19 cm	2nd lead no pix
Presentation of safety award	7 cm	presentation pic of 6 people
Road crash – non-fatal	15 cm	no pix
Assault case at court – man jailed	24 cm	down page story
Assorted fillers		

The length in the example above refers to the length of the copy if the type is set in the standard house style over a standard column width. The art of *casting off* is no longer the essential skill of the sub-editor. Before copy was directly set on computers, subs would get the stories on type-written sheets from the reporters. These would be edited and then *cast-off*: the sub would calculate how many words of copy there were and how much space this would fill at a certain type size. Subs would often keep charts (handy reckoners) detailing the space a certain number of words would fill. Standard 8pt body size over a 10.5 pica-em column might allow 16 words per column centimetre. On that basis 160 words would fill 10 cm and 320 words would take 20 cm. Accurate casting off was important otherwise when the page was put together in the composing room, the story might be shorter than the space allotted, or, worse still, longer. If a story was short, then a small filler would be inserted in the space. One of the regular jobs on the subs desk of a newspaper at the start of the shift would be to send a number of small news items to be set as fillers. They would be used only to fill up gaps on a column where the copy was short.

A column that was over-length would require cuts and this was the job of the stone-sub – a sub who worked on the *stone* (the working area in the composing room). This sub would work with the compositors, making cuts, checking the right material was going on the right page in the right place, that pictures were the right way up and that headlines said what they were supposed to say. The computer has made most of this work superfluous, because the necessary checks can be made by the sub who designed the page. In theory, making cuts on an over-length story should have been easy. The story should have been subbed so that the last paragraph, and if necessary, the penultimate paragraph could just be removed. But of course, it was not always that simple.

Although casting off is no longer an essential skill, having a reasonable idea of the kind of space a story requires still makes the job of designing pages much easier. It is worth finding out how many words will fit into a column centimetre in the standard type of your publication. You will then be able to quickly calculate that a 460 word story will fill 29 cm at, for instance, 16 words per col/cm.

The instructions column in Example 1 above shows the instructions given by the chief sub to the designer. In this case, as the lead story and pictures are potentially good, you will want them to dominate the page. If the story had been weak (the blaze perhaps only a small affair with no-one hurt) then the chief sub might have wanted to give other stories a more equal treatment.

It is not vital that the lead story be placed at the top of the page – this is a tradition that is upheld more by laziness than any other reason. What we are seeking to do is provide the reader with an *entry point* – a way of getting into the page. This entry point could be the heading for the story lead, but is more likely to be a picture. According to research carried out by the Poynter Institute in the US: 'When the reader enters a page, attention is drawn to no predetermined position. Instead . . . the reader's attention focuses first on the dominant visual element' (Garcia and Stark 1991: 26).

This means that if we wish to draw the reader into the page at the bottom or in the middle, we can do so provided we offer the reader a suitable visual cue such as a large and dominant headline or picture or a bright splash of colour. This is a technique that is often carried to extremes on the front of some of the tabloids which will have just a picture and a headline with the copy carried on the following pages.

We traditionally read text from top left to bottom right and some of this habit continues when we read newspapers, but we actually start to read at the entry point.

To return to our example, the house blaze is the main story and there are no other stories for that page that can compete with it for newsworthiness and so there is no reason to break from the tradition of taking the story to the top of the page. We also have some pictures to go with the story and we can use these with the headline to provide a strong entry point to bring the reader straight to the story we want them to read first, because we think it is the most significant.

When designing pages, often the temptation is to run all the stories at similar prominence, but this rarely works well and merely offers flat and uninspiring pages that are difficult for the reader to navigate. If we can't decide which story is the most newsworthy and which the reader ought to look at first, we might as well give up design and run the stories one after another with only a few cross-heads to separate them. By choosing one story to dominate the page and using the other stories to support that, we offer the reader a page that is attractive, logically structured and easy to navigate offering entertainment, information and value for the cover price. That doesn't mean that we have to make all lead stories the same size though. If a story is a big news item, we would give it more display than a lead that was not very interesting. Talking about using the same style of design and weight of lead heading day after day, revolutionary *Daily Mail* editor Mike Randall said: '. . . by slavish adherence to it you cannot avoid the false emphasis it gives. . . . The whole system creates a straightjacket from which you cannot escape' (Hutt 1967: 46).

In this instance, the story is strong (a house blaze is always good copy for a local paper, fire and flood are about the worst disasters that can happen to householder) and there is no problem about making it dominate the page, but sometimes a story is not so strong. We still need to make such a lead dominate the page, but we can make other stories come close to that dominance by running the lead in the centre of the page or down one side, or even by putting it at the bottom of the page. That way we avoid the asymmetricallity of several similarly displayed stories on a page, without allowing the story we have chosen to lead the page to completely dominate the page when other stories are as good. The other stories might not get the display, but they do get good position. We need to develop a hierarchy on pages that assists readers and guides them through the material we are offering.

You should next consider how much space you are going to give the lead story. The average tabloid page is approximately 38 cm deep (although this can vary from 36 cm to 42 cm) with approximately 36 cm depth of useable space. This will often be nominally spread over seven columns. This gives 252 column centimetres of space per page. If we were to give our lead story a heading of two lines over six columns each at 72pt, this would take 36 col/cm of space. A picture of 4 columns by 10 cm deep would take another 40 col/cm and we have 26 cm of copy. A second picture of three columns by 8 cm would add 24 cm and then we need to add 8 cm for bylines, captions and so on. This very basic design (see Figure 6.4) would take 134 col/cm filling 53 per cent of the page – more than half the space available on the page for one story. As you will see from the design, the first column has space under the double column intro. It is tempting to incorporate this space into the lead story display by adding another heading or putting a small picture at the bottom of the double column text area. The alternative is to run some of the filler stories in that space, perhaps boxed off from the lead story.

The design section for this lead story is traditional and straight-forward. However, the two-line heading, double column intro and pic give a clear entry point. The reader's eye is drawn into the pictures, easily follows up to the bold, strong headline and then to the double column intro which is obviously where they are expected to start reading. The captions and bylines are tucked into the space left alongside the three column picture. This copy could be placed to the

Figure 6.4 The visual is started with the lead story

left of the three-column picture and that picture moved to the right by one column, but this will place the captions next to the copy and look ugly. By pulling the smaller picture to the centre of the page and surrounding it by text associated with the story, the entry point is emphasised. The entry point to the story (as opposed to the page) is further emphasised by setting it in bigger and bolder type across two columns. This makes it clear where the reader should go in order to start reading the text. We can ensure the captions stand with the pictures by setting the type in bold ragged right. This will mean the right-hand side of the text would be unjustified and this will put more white space between it and the story on its right. To further separate it, a line can be drawn from the top picture down and then left to the bottom picture surrounding the text and holding it next to the pictures to which it refers.

Having chosen our lead story and page entry point, it is now much easier to determine what to do with the rest of the page. We have a story that the chief sub wants to be second lead (the next most important story on the page) and another picture. There is also a court case. None of these sound particularly attractive. The picture is of an award presentation, important to the participants, but a big yawn to the rest of us. The second lead is a council story – an important matter of record, but not exciting – and the court case is fairly run-of-the-mill.

We need to consider the next entry point. Where do we want the reader to go next? Although the picture of the awards is boring, we are obliged to use it and so it needs to be of a reasonable size. The only place to put something this large is under the lead. We could take the picture right to the bottom of the page, but placing pictures along the edges of pages is rarely a good idea, pictures draw the eye and there is a risk that reader's eye will then slip out of one page onto another. In any case, putting the picture at the bottom would require us putting something in between the lead and the picture, which would be difficult to do. The easiest way around this problem is to put something else at the bottom of the page – an *anchorpiece*; a story spread across the bottom of the page holding the bottom together. A risk of a newspaper page without an anchorpiece is that there are several stories like dangling legs of text at the bottom. This can give the page a frayed look as though it is unravelling. By putting an anchorpiece across the bottom, either boxed or unboxed, we can gather those dangling legs neatly together. The court case is ideal for this (see Figure 6.5). We can spread this story over six columns, setting the text into four or five columns of *bastard* setting. A single line heading across all six columns in a modest size (36pt to 48pt) will firmly hold the bottom of the page together.

The second lead can now be dropped from the top of the page down the right-hand single column (see Figure 6.6). Five lines of 36pt or 42pt should be strong enough (although this will only allow four to five characters, not an easy headline to write – I've only recently forgiven the sub who once asked me to write a six-line heading at three characters per line). This, with the 19 cm of text, will drop to about where the lead story ends. It is worth matching these up, even if it means cutting a few words from the second lead story.

We can now run the awards picture under a six-column single line light heading under the lead (see Figure 6.7). The text can run in the single column space on the bottom far right. We should consider whether the copy would be run in bold or roman or even if it should be set in the caption font. Ragged right is another thing to consider.

Figure 6.5 Now an anchorpiece is added to tie up the bottom of the page

Finally we fill the single column space below the left-hand side of the lead intro with the report on the car accident filling up with as many fillers as we need, to provide a short news-in-brief column down the left hand side. The full page can now be viewed in Figure 6.8. Having drafted it out on paper with pencil does not take that long (an experienced designer would have pencilled in a draft like this in two or three minutes). It takes far longer to explain than to do.

Take a good look at the page: the story count is fine – there are seven items on the page and it is lively and active. Good entry points are provided with the

Figure 6.6   The second lead fills the right-hand column

three pictures. But is the awards picture too big? Does it dominate the page when that should be the lead story's job? Probably not. Although it is fairly dominant, the two pictures above it are stronger. It takes up more space than it is worth, but any smaller and it would be impossible to identify the people in the picture.

However, if the picture had been given too much display, this would have been obvious in the visual. Scribbled out on a piece of paper in only a couple of minutes, it only takes a couple of seconds to screw it up and bin it before replacing it with a sketch that takes account of that discovery. The amount of

Publication: *Journal*   Day: *Tues*   edtn: *First*

Five saved as family escapes home blaze

House plans law set to change

Figure 6.7   The picture story is added. The picture contains 30 faces and so is very wide and shallow

effort invested in the original draft is minimal, and in any case the time is not wasted, because it was possible to go on to produce a better version. But if you had spent up to an hour doing this on computer, laying in the text and sizing the pictures, you would be far less keen to change the page – there would have been too much time and effort invested, but an attempted redesign at this stage would probably fail to produce what's needed. Working with paper and pencil in the first instance to produce quick visuals makes sense and saves effort. Only start laying out on the computer when you are sure you've got it right.

Figure 6.8   The final design with fillers in the column below the lead

FEATURE AND MAGAZINE PAGES

These are not so different from a news page, except that there may only be one piece of text. Again the starting point should be the entry point. This is fairly obvious for us – there is only one story and we want the reader to start at the beginning, but we still need to signal this to the reader by use of the picture and heading. This means the picture must dominate the page and one of the easiest mistakes to make as a beginner is to use too small a picture. Figure 6.9 shows a

Let's singa songa Julia

WOWING them in the West end after a triumphant run in one of TV's favourite soaps, Julia Frost is at the top of her game.

"Life's great for me at the moment," she says, "I can't think how it could get any better."

But this bright new star in the British theatrical firmament is no overnight success. "no," says Julia, "I'm afraid it's slog, slog, slog. You don't get anywhere in the theatrical world without putting in loads of hard work and convincing people you're able to do the job."

Julia started her theatre career after university, where she studied acting. She joined a small theatre group touring schools showing plays and educational material.

Carry on writing loads of material like this, well supported with quotes from the subject and other people who know her.

Carry on writing loads of material like this, well supported with quotes from the subject and other people who know her.

Carry on writing loads of material like this, well supported with quotes from the subject and other people who know her.

Carry on writing loads of material like this, well supported loads of material like this, well sup loads of material like this, well sup with quotes from the subject and other people who know her. Carry on writing loads of material like this, well supported with quotes from the subject and other people loads of material like this, well sup who know her.

Carry on writing loads of material like this, well supported with quotes from the subject and other

Julia Frost (pictured) has stormed the West End in her new muscial "Whistle While You Work". Alison Webster talks to the new star and discovers that over-night success is anything but.

from the subject and other.

Carry on writing loads of material like this, well supported with quotes from the subject and other people who know her well supported with quotes from the subject and other.

Carry on writing loads of material like this, well supported with quotes from the subject and other people who know her.

Carry on writing loads of material like this, well supported with quotes from the subject and other people who know her.

Carry on writing loads of material like this, well supported loads of material like this, well supported with quotes from the subject and other

Carry on writing loads of material like this, well supported with quotes from the subject and other people who know her.

Carry on writing loads of loads of material like this, well supported material like this, well supported with quotes from the subject and other people who know her

Carry on writing loads of material like this, well supported with quotes from the subject and other people who know her

Carry on writing loads loads of material like this, well supported of material like this, well supported with quotes from the subject and other people who know her

Carry on writing loads of material like this, well

Figure 6.9 A feature page. Note the dominance of the picture and how this feeds into the headline to create an unmissable entry point magazine page. It's a 'celebrity-style' feature with an interview and picture. The picture dominates the page and draws the reader in. The heading is also large to clearly identify the entry point and it overlaps the picture. The picture is cut away because the background tells us nothing about the picture, the picture is only of interest because of the facial animation that makes us want to read the story. Cutting away some of the background accentuates this animation. It also allows us to take the hand out into the text, breaking up some of the vertical lines through the page. I cannot show the page in colour, but the picture, which was taken in Italy, is made up of warm sand colours and this colour might well be continued into the heading, perhaps combined with a purple-blue, which is the natural complementary colour. This would emphasise the sandy colour and make it more vibrant and interesting.

The text would then run beneath the heading and around the pictures. The second picture and standfirst would be placed around the bottom of the main picture to break up the text. This page uses a standard four-column grid and without the extra picture, the page would look very flat. Using the picture allows us to start off with a wide intro and then break into a three column setting across the bottom of the page.

Dropping the pictures so deep allows us to put a significant amount of text in without it appearing to be overwhelming. I think the text is just about short enough not to need help, but you could consider putting drop caps in halfway down the first column and halfway through the last column. Instead of using drop caps a crosshead might also help break the longer first column.

Often a feature is long enough to go onto a second page or even more. You might then have to take a decision about whether to run the copy on or break it up. Readers will happily follow a feature through three or four pages, but it might be better to split the feature so that the main text can run through all the pages, forcing the reader to stick with it, but with sidebar and boxed pieces of text placed in the pages to allow the reader to break off and look at something slightly different.

Story counts

Story counts are an important consideration when designing pages. The correct story count for each page should be a careful balance between interest, size of page and material available. There should be a good balance between text and image and other design devices such as headings, captions and other display text. A feature page or magazine page may only have one story on the page. This needs to be carefully balanced with image and display. A news page for a newspaper or magazine will have a much higher story count. This will vary according to the liveliness required. A page with a major news story could have only one story on the page. A major UK train crash, the abduction of children, a major disaster could all be stories that require not just a page of their own, but a number of pages. However, the story would probably be broken up into a number of different pieces of text so that inside pages at least had several stories, headlines and pictures in order to maintain interest.

Not only does this allow the stories from different reporters to be kept separate, but also allows for the views of different witnesses and different angles and positions on the story. By keeping the story count per page reasonable – even when it is all the same story – we maintain reader interest. The story count on a tabloid page will traditionally be 5–7 and on a broadsheet it could be as high as 12. On a magazine news page, particularly one where none of the stories are especially strong, the story count could be even higher.

Essentially, if the stories are not strong in their own right, then providing a high story count will often get round this problem. Readers enjoy a column of nibs (news in brief) as much as one strong story. If the stories for the page are not strong, then cut them drastically and keep the story count high.

Headings as display

Headings play a major part in any design. They signal entry points and lead the reader's eye around the page. Fashions for headings have changed over the years. The old-fashioned multi-decker heading has gone to be replaced with more multi-purpose headings. A multi-deck heading is one with several headings each different to the next and this should not be confused with the number of lines a heading has. A four-line heading is not the same as a four-deck heading, which is four separate headings relating to the same story. Hutt attributes this development to the likes of W.T. Stead and T.P. O'Connor whom he labels the 'true pioneers of the New Journalism' (Hutt 1967: 36). The change to photosetting and web-offset opened the way for even more flexibility in display text. Headings were no longer limited to columns, different sizes and shapes could be set easily. The old-fashioned decks set 'full out and centred turn' (ibid.: 35) could now be set flush left or centred and required wording to be carefully thought through to fit the space allocated. This meant that headings were no longer just a part of the story, but while being involved with it, were also separate to it – an active and dynamic part of the process of drawing the reader into the story.

Headings can now be used across different column widths. One heading could be used to link two stories, for instance, while another will pick up one element of a story and a further sub-heading will break the columns beneath the intro.

When designing pages, you should try to avoid too much heading. Apart from taking up valuable space, too many headings means inevitable clashes making the page look ugly. Headings should be kept from other headings by text, rules or pictures. Avoid running headings for different stories together. Sometimes it is unavoidable as in a single and double column down the page. Then you can try to ensure they do not clash by using different sizes, different fonts or for instance, by parting two similar double column headings from each other with a boxed single-column light heading. Headings should be signs to the entry point of a story so any heading which is away from the intro should be avoided. Only if there is only one story on the page can a heading that is split from the story ever hope to succeed. Even here it is unlikely to work well.

Reversing headings to set them white on black or place them on a colour tone patch can often help lift a headline away from the rest of the page and this is also a useful technique for emphasis. Patches of colour are identified by the Poynter Institute's research as good entry points (Garcia and Stark 1991: 25). But, as with all devices, they should not be used to excess. There should be a good reason for more than one tone or reverse heading on a page. More than one or two makes the page look like a patchwork and loses the novelty that you had hoped to obtain. Beware of using different typefaces for headings. All your heading type should be in the same family with the possible exception of one or two headlines in something completely different as a *kicker*. Papers with serif headline faces often use a gothic (sans serif) face as a *kicker*, again to add emphasis and variety. Gothic-faced papers will use a semi-sans typeface such as Cooper Black. This is a heavy face in which the serifs are so stylised as if not to appear. It works well with gothic faces, providing variety, without looking out of place. The watchword should always be to use *kickers* sparingly, as with any other device, a little goes a long way.

The shape of headings, particularly on the lead story, does a lot to help the design of the page. The main picture and the lead heading are the two most likely entry points for a reader and therefore, if you can get them to work together, they are likely to draw the reader into the page just where you want them. There are a number of shapes that can be applied to a lead heading. Multi-line headings can be used: anything up to five lines on a three or four column heading. *Streamers* – headings that go across the full page – tied in with sub-headings over several lines but fewer columns can also make attractive page starts, especially if they are tied in with a good picture. Another device is the *strapline*: a heading above the lead heading in type of about one third or a quarter of that of the main heading. Straplines are particularly useful where several pictures and several pieces of text all need to be tied together (see Figure 6.10).

Drivers 'distracted' by roadside activity

Two killed in M-way pile up

By JOHN SMITH

TWO PEOPLE were killed and four others injured in a multiple pile up on the M62 yesterday.

The accident happened in fog near the Huddersfield turn off. Police believe that one of the drivers may have been distracted by activity at a building close to the motorway.

The two killed were Mr John Bates, of High St, Chorley and Mr Peter Sims of Bassenthwaite Lane, Oldham.

The injured were taken to hospital but were later released. They were said to be suffering from shock and minor cuts and bruises.

A police spokesman said: "Lorries were being loaded under bright lights at factories alongside the motorway and we believe that one of the drivers might have been momentarily distracted. With the fog so thick, a moment is all that it would have taken."

Four cars were involved in the accident and police were surprised that more were not drawn in. The spokesman said: "Luckily, the accident happened in the inside lane and so other drivers were able to avoid the crash fairly easily. It was also easy for us to remove the cars from the carriageway very quickly."

Police were on the scene in just a few minutes, according to witnesses and were able to prevent any further carnage.

The accident happened at 6.30am and so traffic was relatively light. The early morning fog lifted later on

The scene of the accident shortly after the crash.

The dice with death we 'take for granted'

Figure 6.10 A strapline above a multi-line heading with a double column intro

PICTURES ON A PAGE

The pictures on a page are as important, if not more important than the headings. Preferably you should work on the two together, but if this is difficult, plan where you intend to put the pictures first and then work text and headings around them. Pictures, as I have said, are the most likely entry point for a reader. Provided a picture has been well chosen and appropriately edited, you will need to make it a reasonable size in order to ensure it has the necessary impact. Harold Evans's seminal book about pictures (Evans 1978: 3) has a picture of an aeroplane taking off. Only on close inspection can you see a stowaway falling from the jet's wheel housing. This is a picture that needs to be used in a large size in order to see the stowaway in the context of the jet.

Nearly all pictures worth using need to be of a reasonable size. The average holiday snap these days is printed at least 15 cm by 10 cm, and that is on high quality photographic paper. If you are considering using a smaller picture (other than a mugshot), you should be asking yourself whether the picture is worth using at all. It also depends on what the picture is about; a passport-style picture of someone named in the story could be used as small as 3 cm by 4 cm, but any picture with several faces would need to be large enough for the reader to be able to easily identify the faces. A picture with small detail important to the story would need to be big enough for the reader to see that detail easily. This could mean that some photographs with lots of people or a wealth of detail would need to be six or seven columns wide. You would then have to justify to yourself that a picture that large is worth using. The wrong decision would be to use it in any case even if small – that just ensures you have a picture that no reader will be able to see and the space would be completely wasted. Either use pictures large enough to give them their full dramatic impact and to allow the reader to see what's in the picture, or don't use them at all.

It is possible to use more than one picture with a story and often this is the only way to show the full detail. When working with several pictures on the same story try to get some variation. Aim for different shapes and sizes so that you are able to make that part of the page appear livelier. The exception to this is if you want to use several pictures as a single block, in which case you could keep the sizes the same and place them alongside each other. You might also want to use several pictures for the purpose of comparison, and here again you might also use them in a series in the same size.

TEXT

Once the headings and the pictures are placed on the page, you need to start laying in the text. Most of this will be set in the standard body size for your publication, whatever that is. However, varying the type size and how it is presented will liven up the page and add emphasis to sections of the story. This is particularly important if the story is of any length, a feature page for example. Whether it is for a newspaper or a magazine, the longer runs of text require careful handling to avoid presenting the reader with large areas of indigestible grey.

Intros as entry points

The first variation that can be made in the type size and presentation is in the entry point of the text. You should already have directed the reader to this point with headings and pictures, but it doesn't hurt to emphasise the start for the reader. This is often done by setting the *intro* in a larger type, possibly bold (see Figure 6.11). Sometimes, if the story is run over more than one column, or in the more flexible style of a magazine, the intro can be set over a wider measure than the rest of the text. This often allows a sub-heading or a byline to be set in the run of text (see Figures 6.11 and 6.12). Magazines can handle the intro right across the page, if the type is set large enough, but newspapers rarely go above 14pt for their intros and this tends to limit you to three or four columns (40 ems maximum) (see Figure 6.13). Anything wider rarely has the depth required to sustain it and tends to look thin and unimportant. It also becomes difficult to read.

Sometimes a publication will even set the intro in a different font – sans serif for instance, to emphasise the start (see Figure 6.12). It is usual to set the first or first two words of a story in capitals. This again helps emphasise the entry point for the story.

Running and shaping text

After the intro, the main run of text needs to be considered. Long runs of text usually need to be set over a wider measure than short runs (see Chapter 9). With modern computer setting it is also possible to wrap text around pictures and other items, often in quite complicated shapes. This is a technique (like most tricks) that should be used sparingly, but can add emphasis to a picture or graphic and brighten up a page. Text can be run over pictures and graphics to add emphasis, but should also be used sparingly. Unless the text is set in a fairly large size, any underlying image is likely to make the text more difficult to read.

Nearly all longer stories need to be set in multi-columns. It is difficult to make hard and fast rules in design, but once you start moving into multi-columns rather than a single column drop, then it is best to avoid dropping the story too deep. Better to have four columns 10 cm deep than two columns of 20 cm. This

TWO PEOPLE were killed and four others injured in a multiple pile up on the M62 yesterday.

The accident happened in fog near the Huddersfield turn off. Police believe that one of the drivers may have been distracted by activity at a building close to the motorway.

By John Smith

The two killed were Mr John Bates, of High St, Chorley and Mr Peter Sims of BassenthwaiteLane, Oldham.

The injured were taken to hospital but were later released. They were said to be suffering from shock and minor cuts and bruises.

A police spokesman said:

"Lorries were being loaded under bright lights at factories alongside the motorway and we believe that one of the drivers might have been momentarily distracted. With the fog so thick, a moment is all that it would have taken."

Four cars were involved in

Figure 6.11 A standard double-column intro, with the byline placed in the shoulder to allow the second column to stand clear of the intro

TWO PEOPLE were killed and four others injured in a multiple pile up on the M62 yesterday.

The accident happened in fog near the Huddersfield turn off. Police believe that one of the drivers may have been distracted by activity at a building close to the motorway.

The two killed were Mr John Bates, of High St, Chorley and Mr Peter Sims of BassenthwaiteLane, Oldham.

Driver's fatal distraction

The injured were taken to hospital but were later released. They were said to be suffering from shock and minor cuts and bruises.

A police spokesman said: "Lorries were being loaded under bright lights at factories alongside the motorway and we believe that one of the drivers might have been momentarily distracted. With the fog so thick, a moment is all that it would have taken."

Four cars were involved in the accident and police were

surprised that more were not drawn in. The spokesman said: "Luckily, the accident happened in the inside lane and so other drivers were able to avoid the crash fairly easily. It was also easy for us to remove the cars from the carriageway

Figure 6.12 A similar idea, but this time with a secondary heading. Note the use of a sans serif font for the first para

"TWO PEOPLE were killed and four others injured in a multiple pile up on the M62 yesterday.

The accident happened in fog near the Huddersfield turn off. Police believe that one of the drivers may have been distracted by activity at a building close to the motorway."

It's a familiar story. High speeds, poor driving conditions and a moment's distraction. All too often these days, drivers become blaze about the lethal weapons they control everyday.

Many drivers travel huge distances in a day, driving for hours at a time on smooth motorways in cars that are built for comfort. We forget that if you were to take us out of our air conditioned armchair, away from the hi-fi CD player and the power steering, we wouldn't last five minutes on a motorway. Tons of motor

Are today's cars too luxurious? Motoring writer John Smith worries about our 'lethal lounges'.

car or lorry rip up and down this highway at speeds that could saw your arm off without even slowing the vehicle, if you

were to foolishly try to impede its passage. We too are travelling at fantastic speeds, yet it is all too easy to succumb to the

Figure 6.13 A triple-column intro, this time with a standfirst tucked into the shoulder. Running three columns of type immediately under the intro risks confusing the reader doesn't mean that two columns of 20 cm or longer should never be used, just that you should always look to see if you can spread the story wider.

Text presentation

Once the text is laid onto the page, the work does not end there. The options available for dealing with the text are almost endless.

One of the standard choices is to tabulate copy or put it into tables. This is ideal for sports results, league tables, TV listings and so on. Any setting that is not narrative but a list of information in a standardised form should be considered for setting in this way. Tabulation allows you to set up columns within the column of your text to line up items of the same sort. Tables allow for something similar, but in a boxed format.

Even if the text is a straight run of narrative, you might want to add emphasis to certain sections, either for editorial reasons – the paragraph you are emphasising is of particular importance – or for design reasons – it's there to keep the reader's interest and to give them a marker through the copy. Markers are useful because if the reader becomes distracted, there is a marker to remind them of where they were.

This emphasis can be added with drop caps, indented paragraphs, underlined text, emboldened text, italicised text, or by increasing the size of a paragraph (see Figure 8.12 for examples).

OTHER TYPES OF DISPLAY

As well as being part of the story, other text elements can be used as design devices to break up long runs of text, separate stories and to split pictures from each other and from inappropriate text. For instance, captions can split a picture from another picture or from text. Captions need to be used carefully. The convention is to place a caption below the picture and you need to think carefully before doing anything else. Readers find it extremely irritating to locate a caption that is not beneath the picture. They want to find out who is in a picture but the sub has decided to tuck it away on the other side of the page or put it in the text. It is possible to run the caption alongside the picture rather than beneath it, sometimes it is even turned through 90° to run up the side of the photo (see Figure 9.5). It is also possible to pierce the picture to insert a caption so that it covers a part of the picture that is otherwise a waste of space.

Bylines are another device that can break up an area of text or pictures. Bylines can be used in the shoulder of an intro to give the break into the second column. They can be used at the end of an introductory paragraph, or they can be large areas of display. They can be included in standfirsts, with or without a picture to make a large area of display. This would certainly be how a celebrity byline might be used. An article by David Beckham on being England Captain in a football magazine, for instance, or a newspaper's sports pages, would use a very large picture byline/standfirst that might also incorporate the heading: 'Playing for my country – David Beckham on the boyhood dream of leading the England squad' (see Figure 9.3 for an example).

SOME DOS AND DON'TS OF DESIGN

Setting out golden rules is a proven way to trip over your own good intentions but there are some things one should always consider doing when designing pages and so I offer my own golden rules:

- Choose your entry point with care and make it the focal point of the page.
- Break up long stories into easily manageable articles linked together by design.
- Use pictures and graphics wherever possible.
- Break up type to add interest.
- Consider using subheads and crossheads to add emphasis to sections of the text.
- Consider using bulleted pars, drop letters and bold pars to add emphasis.
- Keep things simple and easy to follow.
- Consider carefully how long each article should be, depending on your readership profile.
- Try to avoid clashing with adverts. Ads with large areas of halftone should be cordoned off using text. Text-based adverts could be put next to pictures.
- Consider how best to get over the information. For instance, an annotated aerial picture may do more to describe the scene of an accident than pages of text could hope to do. It will be the designer's job to arrange for the text and pictures to be turned into a diagram.
- Consider using just parts of a picture, or cutting out the image or overlaying it with type.
- Ensure that there is a suitable amount of white space around the headlines and any other elements.
- Ensure that there is always a caption beneath any picture. Readers get very irritated if they can't find the caption to a picture.

- Emphasise your entry point with larger intro type, bold faces, drop letters etc.

- Ensure that the strength of your stories is reflected in the design.

- The reader should be in no doubt about where the story continues after it has ended in one column.

- Be imaginative in how you deal with the elements of a page.

Similarly there are things that it is wise to avoid. Although it is alright to do these things occasionally if you've thought things through properly, generally you should try to avoid:

- Running headlines over adverts. Always break the space with text or pictures. If the space above a run of adverts is too small to be useful, don't be afraid to give it up and float the ads to the top or ask the advertising dept. to fill the space. Anything less than 6 cm is going to give you problems.

- Running a headline next to another headline unless the stories are connected or unless you have some way of ensuring they are not connected such as column rules or by using very different styles and sizes of font.

- Covering the page with lots of different typefaces. Too much variation will end up just looking a mess. It is best to limit yourself to one font and using varieties of it.

- Using cut outs on a picture just for the sake of it. Whether the picture is cut away from its background or a section is cut out, it will lose context and start to look isolated. A cut out used without a good reason usually looks ridiculous because it is clear you are trying to edit the picture and the reader will wonder why.

- Turning copy to another page. It's a great way of ensuring the reader loses interest in the story.

7

Master pages, templates and style sheets

Master pages, templates and style sheets are devices within the main desktop publishing software packages aimed at making life easier for publishers. There are several desktop publishing software packages available, but the one most often used for professional publishing is Quark Xpress, although Aldus's Pagemaker or Indesign are used in some places. Aldus Indesign and Quark Xpress are now very similar packages doing the same job in much the same way. Pagemaker does the same thing slightly differently. Those who like it claim it is more flexible and more intuitive to use, those who prefer Quark claim that Pagemaker is more complicated.

Most designers are obliged to use whatever software package their employer has invested in and for those working in publishing, this is usually Quark Xpress running on Apple Macs. It's doubtful that one system is better than any other all of the time – the key is always how good you are at designing publications and at getting the best out of the system you are obliged to use.

THE IMPORTANCE AND PURPOSE OF MASTER PAGES AND TEMPLATES

Master pages are pages that are not actually printed out but ones that keep general information common to all pages in a publication linked to the master page. They are different from templates or copy pages in that they can be altered at any time during publishing and the changes will be reflected in the final publication and on every page of the publication linked to the master page.

There are usually two master pages per publication, one for the left hand pages and one for the right. Any standard material that runs through the whole publication can be placed on a master page and it will appear on every page in the publication that is linked to that master page. So, if you were to put the page number on the top right hand corner of the right-hand master page, that page number would then appear on every page. Since it is possible to instruct the

DTP software to automatically match the page number as printed to the actual number of that page, this is an easy way to insert page numbers, or other header material.

Master pages are good for placing header material, footer material and any other logos, guidelines or material that go on every page throughout the publication. For every page you work on, you can then select, whether it picks up the master page and which master page it selects.

Templates

As well as master pages, which can be used to set up headers and footers and regularly used material, it is also possible to set up templates. These are pages that are standardised and allow the editor or designer to select a style of page which is already part-designed. This saves a lot of work and potential for mistakes. If a standard tabloid page is 38.6 cm by 29.2 cm with 12 mm margins, then it is easier to call up a standard tabloid page, than to remember this detail every time you start a new page.

A template will first define the page size and margins. A newspaper might produce in both broadsheet (for the main publication) and tabloid (for the supplements). Templates would be required for both sizes of pages. The margins would also need to be fixed on the templates.

Next the template will contain the standard number of columns required. This might mean that a news page in a tabloid newspaper page would have seven columns. The feature pages might have only six columns and the broadsheet news pages might have nine columns. Each column would have a space between it and the next column and again the template would fix this according to the standard decided by the publication designer. Templates should carry all the information about a page that a sub-editor will require. The sub-editor can then call up the appropriate page and start designing.

The templates can also be extended to pick up information that always appears on standard pages such as TV listings, entertainments pages and so on. This means that the TV listings template, for instance, will already have appropriate headings such as BBC1, BBC2 etc., in place. The standard space for reviews and pictures will already have frames placed on the page so the sub-editor can quickly insert the text and pictures and send the page.

The only risk with templates is that many publications are starting to look very similar. If the editor decides to have a template for each news and feature page that already carry frames for headlines, stories and pictures so that the same design is always used, then there is a risk that each edition will start to look the same and news stories will be presented at the same strength regardless of their merit. Although computers and modern printing methods should give the designer more freedom, the use of templates has in fact often brought about a sameness to pages that is unfortunate. While using the same template for the TV listings day after day makes sense, always using the same design for page three will soon bore readers.

This is not to oppose the tidy look of a page that is adhering to the publication's house style, nor to not welcome the savings brought by standardised pages where the margins, columns and artwork are automatically put onto the page, but it is to deprecate the unwillingness, usually caused by lack of time, to use that framework imaginatively by tweaking the style where it will advance the design or by altering the standard templates for reasons other than necessity. As well as fixing such items as margins and columns, a good template also includes a style sheet.

Style sheets

Style sheets are used in major DTP packages and in word-processing packages. Anyone skilled in using one of the major word processing packages may already be familiar with style sheets and their use in DTP packages is identical. Style sheets allow the user to preformat certain types of paragraph. For instance, the standard body type that will be used in the publication can be called 'body text' and its font, size, leading and paragraph characteristics can then be pre-determined. Assume, for instance, that the publication is using Nimrod as its body type. The designer may have decided that body style would be: 8pt Nimrod on an 8.5pt body, justified with standard kerning tables and a UK English dictionary. There might be 3pt of space before each paragraph and the first line of each paragraph would be indented by an em space. Hyphenation rules would be pre-decided. All of this can then be pre-formatted by defining a new style or editing an existing one. There will then be a style called 'body text' which can be easily applied to sections of text. Open the style palette in your software and click the style called body text and that style will be instantly applied to the paragraph in which your cursor is sitting. If you want to apply the style to several paragraphs, just select them and click on the style. In order to load copy into the frame already to style, the style sheet can be selected when the copy frame is drawn onto the page. The copy will then be set in that style as it is imported.

There is no real practical limit to the number of style sheets that can be predefined and it would be normal for a publication to have predefined style sheets for all standard type elements: body text, intros, bylines, standfirsts, captions, headlines, crossheads, *side-heads* and so on. (See Figure 7.1.)

Figure 7.1 Style sheets on a page make-up system. Menu 1 (top right) shows the styles. Menu 2 allows the user to define the styles. Menu 3 allows editing choices and menus 4 and 5 edit font and paragraph styles

Most publications set up the style sheets right at the beginning of the publication design process to ensure that subs use the pre-determined styles available.

Each templated page should have a style sheet attached that keeps the standard house style, but also introduces any special styles for that page. The TV listings page, for instance, might have fonts and styles not used on other pages and these should be available in the style sheet. If templates are useful (and they are) then style sheets are indispensable. To be able to quickly click on a series of paragraphs and then select a style and click on that, converting a block of type neatly and quickly to the appropriate style is a real time-saver. Time spent developing style sheets is never wasted and always repays itself during the lifetime of a publication.

If ever you get to set up a new publication, do make sure your style sheets cover all the main options your house style is going to allow the designers.

8

Typography

Type is one of the most important design elements of any newspaper or magazine but one that is often overlooked – particularly by the novice. Type plays a major part in the look of any publication. Subtle and imperceptible though it might be to the untrained eye, the face used in a publication plays a direct part in the way we perceive the published words.

To take an extreme example, if we were to publish in Old English characters, readers would perceive what was written in an entirely different way to a publication set in some frivolous art nouveau face. (See Figure 8.1 for a comparison of different fonts.)

A newspaper set entirely in Zapf Chancery would look extremely odd – this is the font of treasure maps and aging documents, not a modern, forward-looking newspaper. It is not easy to read and impedes the eye, its message being contained more in the font style than the words.

A newspaper set entirely in Shelley would also look extremely odd. Elegant and stylish, this font would be at home on an invitation to a garden party, but not alerting us to the death and carnage of the latest terrorist outrage.

Figure 8.1 Fonts for different purposes

In the days of letterpress, there were other factors involved in the choice of font. The actual process of printing meant that great care had to be taken over the choice of type to ensure image clarity. Letterpress is a contact process with the type hammering into the paper at high speed. Only a font that could stand up to those pressures and still print legibly without the 'e's and 'o's filling with ink or the delicate serifs dropping off was of any use. Whole groups of type, called the legibility group, were designed expressly to provide a text type that would print true and be highly readable despite the rigours of the printing process. Fonts such as Ionic, Corona and Paragon took over from the earlier Times roman faces. Each of them had different attributes but all of them tried to balance various factors: reproduction; colour; body size; readability.

Modern computer setting and web-offset lithography allow us much more freedom to choose whatever font we want. The type is no longer subject to the damaging punishment of the press and delicate insubstantial fonts can be used if we want.

However, for most newspapers and magazines, we need to choose a font that will aid the reader as much as possible. It is our job as designers to ensure that the fonts we choose to use are as helpful as possible to the readers so that they can absorb as much of what has been written as is possible in the time available to them. If they become aware of the font, we are probably not doing our job properly.

WHAT IS TYPE?

Type is a method of converting language into symbols that are readily understood by those trained to read. English uses a Roman alphabet and characters, and while this is far from the only alphabet or set of symbols used in the world, it is one that many people can decipher.

Whatever alphabet is used, however, there are two requirements:

1. that there is a symbol produced (or implied) using some form of ink or paint;

2. that there is a space for the character to live in that is not inked.

Both of these requirements are as important as each other and we forget that at our peril. It is the contrast between the symbol and the space in which it is placed that makes reading either easy or difficult. For instance, a light green character on a light blue background is not easy to read and may well be impossible for someone who is colour blind. The art director of a men's magazine who chooses to print green type on a pink background will be upset when scores of readers ring to complain about what they see as a blank page because they are colour blind (a significant minority of men are colour blind). Even those who are not colour blind will not enjoy the experience because it will be difficult to make out the characters. While this might just be acceptable for one or two words – a heading or caption, say; over several thousand words, most readers would soon give up.

Even limiting the colours to black and white requires care. Research by Starch in the 1920s (cited in Tinker 1963: 129) shows that black type on a white background was read 42 per cent faster than white type on a dark grey background. In another study by Paterson and Tinker (cited in Tinker 1963: 130) white on black was read 10.5 per cent slower than black on white. The black on white was preferred by 77.7 per cent of the readers. Figure 8.2 shows some variants on the colour of the paper – see how this varies how easy the text is to read.

When one of my newspaper offices first moved over to computers, there was much concern about the health and safety repercussions of working on screen all day. It was possible for the user to decide how their screen displayed, using either black characters on a white background or white characters on a black background. It is no coincidence that while a lot of reporters happily wrote white on black (because we had been told this would lead to less glare and therefore be safer), most sub-editors changed to black on white. Subs do much more reading than reporters and so legibility is much more important.

Figure 8.2 Paper colour is as important as ink

The shape of the type itself is also important. When we are reading we need to able to quickly identify both the characters that we are reading and the words that those characters make up. We read by identifying word shapes and good readers will identify up to three or four words in one scan. Being able to quickly identify the characters that make up those words is vital. Try deciphering someone's handwriting in order to see how important the shape of letters can be. Only if the type chosen is well-designed and reproduced clearly in the publication will the reader be able to get the best experience.

For this reason, type is much more stylised than is perhaps realised. Moves to simplify type often make it only more difficult to read. Type was historically cast in metal (see Figure 8.3) and much of its terminology comes from this history. There are names for all the different parts of the type, but we only need to be aware that the size of type is determined by the metal block on which it is cast and that type has descenders, ascenders, serifs and an x-height. See Figure 8.4 for details.

Figure 8.3 Metal type. Note that it is a mirror image and that the body of the type is larger than the actual typeface

Figure 8.4   Type and its parts

What is a font?

A font is a single design of type, usually available in a range of different styles. This family of type often means that a type from the same font can be in roman, bold, italic, bold italic, condensed, extended, lower case, small capitals, capitals and so on. This means that even if you have decided to only use one font in your designs, there is still plenty of opportunity to adjust the way the type presents. A bold heading will look very different to a light (or roman) heading even in the same font. Choosing to present it in italic or extended can also make a huge difference.

Measuring type

Type in the UK and US is measured in point sizes (the European continent uses the didot system where the points are known as Ciceros). The point system is a measuring system in its own right so comparisons with other measuring systems are just that, but there are approximately 72 points to the inch (28.34 to the centimetre). It needs to be remembered that the type measurement system was developed for use with metal type that you could actually see and measure. Since this type was cast in metal, the actual printing face was mounted on top of a metal block and it was this block (or body) that gave type its size, not the actual size of the letters. This means that it is very difficult to measure the size of type once it is printed on the page as it is the space in which the type lives that we actually measure, not the symbol printed on the page. Added to this, publications shrink slightly after printing. So that what was set as 60pt might only be 57.6pt after printing. Figure 8.5 shows the variety of type size.

Figure 8.5 (opposite)   Type is measured in *points*

8pt type - as the type gets smaller, so more words will fit on the line. This 8pt will be used for body type.

10pt type - as the type gets smaller, so more words will fit on the line. This 10pt will l

12pt type - as the type gets smaller, so more words will fit on the line.

14pt type - as the type gets smaller, so more words will fit on

18pt type - as the type gets smaller, so more words

24pt type - as the type gets smaller,

30pt type - as the type gets

36pt type - as the type

48pt type - as the

60pt type - as

72pt type -

Things can be further confused when additional space is inserted between the lines of type. This is know as *leading* (pronounced 'ledding') because it used to be produced by inserting strips of lead or brass of the appropriate thickness between the lines of type. Nowadays, of course, the computer produces the gap, but most software programs will still refer to the space produced as leading. This means that the size of the character and the space in which it lives are the product of several factors:

- the design of the font;

- the size of the font;

- the leading used with the font.

Points are used for vertical measurement in type. For horizontal measurement the pica-em is used. A pica is an old-fashioned name for 12pt type. Before the point system came into general use, type had names for sizes: Pearl (5pt); Ruby (5½pt); Nonpareil, pronounced nonprul, (6pt); Minion (7pt); Brevier (8pt). Bourgeousi, pronounced 'burjoyce' (9pt); Long Primer (10pt); Pica (12pt). Only Pica (pronounced 'piker') has survived into modern usage.

An em-quad is the square of the size of type being used. In the old days of metal type, it was actually a square block of metal, measuring the square of the type used. This means that an em-quad is not a particular size; one can have an eight point em-quad or a 24pt em-quad. However, for measuring the width of columns, pictures and other horizontal measurements, we use pica-ems – a 12pt measure. This is often abbreviated to pica (in the US) or to em (in the UK). We use ems (sometimes called *muttons*) as a measure to indent type. If a paragraph is indented (starts with a space) then it is probably indented by a mutton – an em space – or a *nut* (an en or half an em).

Some books claim that an em is the width of a standard 12pt roman letter 'm' as this is the widest character (Giles and Hodgson 1996: 30; Quinn 2001: 81). This seems unlikely as no character 'm' I've ever measured is as wide as the type size it's set in, nor is it an explanation that appears in any of the older books on typography, but it is a handy explanation for its name.

What is leading?

Leading is additional space inserted between lines of type. Imagine that you are writing notes on a standard A4 lined notepad. The space offered by the pad

Figure 8.6 (opposite) Leading can be considered as a reporter's notebook. The typesize might vary, but the distance between the lines remains the same

Your writing might be an average size
and fit well on a pad of lined paper.
But someone else might write in a
larger face and so the type would
not fit the page.

Another person's writing might be quite small and would fit easily
into the lines left by the writing pad, making their copy looking
very different to yours. It would also allow much more
writing to be fitted into the same space - more difficult to
read, but much more economic.

Another person's writing
might be quite large and
would need to be double
spaced or it would not fit.

between the lines remains constant, but you could choose to write in very large or very small letters (see Figure 8.6). If you wrote small, there would be more space between the lines of script. If you wrote large, there would be very little room. Adding space between the lines by leading, has a similar effect, adding or removing space between the lines of type. If, using my notepad analogy, you decided to double space your writing, writing only on every other line, it would give the effect of inserting lead to the value of one of the lines.

White space and leading

White space is vitally important in the design of newspapers and magazines and is vital to the way the type looks and behaves. Just as one would judge a person partly by the house in which they live or the car they drive, one is also influenced not just by the type, but also the space in which it lives. The amount of space allowed to a type not only affects the way we interpret the message the type contains but it also influences how easy the type is to read. Tinker (1963) quotes a number of studies, one by Paterson and Tinker (1940) in particular, that shows a little leading is a good thing as far as legibility is concerned. Adding 2pts of lead to an 8pt type improves legibility by 5 per cent. Interestingly, any increase of leading beyond this does not appear to improve legibility according to Tinker (1963: 93).

However, just because thicker leading than two points does not improve legibility, that doesn't mean it doesn't have other effects. Type with a lot of leading would inevitably have a lot of white space around it. This block of type would look unhurried and uncluttered giving an impression of authority and gravitas. A traditional font such as Times Roman is often combined with plenty of white space by the broadsheets in order to give an impression of thoughtfulness and authority. A tabloid, on the other hand, usually wants to give the impression of brashness, immediacy and liveliness. Tabloids tend to use fonts with large x-heights and minimum white space (see Figure 8.7).

Look in a couple of newspapers to compare adverts. Adverts have to say a lot in very few words and so the font used is of crucial importance to reinforce the message or even add a completely different message. Copy in adverts from banks and insurance companies are often set with plenty of leading and space around the text. They want to give an impression of authority and trustworthiness. An electrical retailer of the 'stack 'em high, sell 'em cheap variety' on the other hand, wants to give an impression of haste, that special offers are being snapped up by bargain hunters. If you don't get to the store today, it might be too late. This is achieved by adverts that are cramped with information, prices and pictures. The adverts don't say it, indeed they often mention helpful staff ready to talk you through the product, but the message in the spacing is intended to

12pt times new roman set
on a 12pt body. This is
a setting that keeps the type
close together.
12pt times new roman set
on a 12pt body. This is
a setting that keeps the type
close together.
12pt times new roman set
on a 12pt body. This is
a setting that keeps the type
close together.
12pt times new roman set
on a 12pt body. This is
a setting that keeps the type
close together.
12pt times new roman set
on a 12pt body. This is
a setting that keeps the type
close together.

12pt times new roman set
on an 18pt body. This puts
a reasonable amount of
space in between the type.
12pt times new roman set
on an 18pt body. This puts
a reasonable amount of
space in between the type.
12pt times new roman set
on an 18pt body. This puts
a reasonable amount of
space in between the type.
12pt times new roman set
on an 18pt body. This puts

12pt times new roman set
on a 14pt body. This puts
a reasonable amount of
space in between the type
without it appearing to
be overspaced.
12pt times new roman set
on a 14pt body. This puts
a reasonable amount of
space in between the type
without it appearing to
be overspaced.
12pt times new roman set
on a 14pt body. This puts
a reasonable amount of
space in between the type
without it appearing to

12pt times new roman set
on a 24pt body. This
double spaces the lines
and gives a very airy,
authoritative feel.

12pt times new roman set
on a 24pt body. This
double spaces the lines
and gives a very airy,
authoritative feel.

Figure 8.7 Leading (the space between lines of type) can have a dramatic effect on the message give the reader the feeling of a busy market place brimming with bargains that need to be snapped up immediately or they will be lost to some other customer.

USING TYPE IN DESIGN

There are five main families of type: old style, transitional, modern, Egyptian and contemporary that represent the development of type over the past 350 years (Craig 1980: 31). Modern types have been with us since the middle of the last century. However, from a design point of view, a better categorisation of type is old style, modern, slab serif, sans serif, script and decorative.

Old style is the design of type used at the start of printing and representing the style of writing prevalent at the time. Scribes used quills and therefore the type was made up of a series of thick and thin strokes. This was mimicked in the type. Old style also has serifs – the little curlicues identifiable on fonts such as Times New Roman.

Modern types maintained the thick and thin strokes and the serifs but became much squarer and blockier as the need to carve or cast the type took precedence over the need to match the style of contemporary scribes.

Sans serif fonts (as their name suggests) do not have the little curlicues at the end of the strokes. Nor do they normally have a mix of thick and thin strokes, although they can. They look even more modern and are simple and unadorned.

Scripts are designed to look like handwriting and are often used to mimic handwriting on invitations and printed matter that is designed to look more personal or elegant. Decorative fonts cover a wide range and are there to have fun with. You wouldn't normally use a decorative font to set more than a few words – they are usually very difficult to read. However, they can add emphasis to a headline or caption.

Serif fonts are normally used for the body text of a newspaper or magazine. There is some debate about why this is. Tinker (1963: 64) claims that a sans serif font is read as rapidly as a seriffed font, although readers prefer serifs. He also accepts that 'The legibility of certain letters . . . can be improved by more judicious use of serifs . . .' (ibid.: 42). Shipcott (1994: 46) claims that serifs do improve legibility, but does not cite a source for this. Either way, it seems that readers prefer serifs and find a seriffed font easier to read. Personally, I think Tinker is right and that the serifs seem to help us identify certain characters a little better, the eye seems to float along the top of the line making reading much easier. Another point about seriffed fonts is that they are much more likely to use thick and thin strokes to add emphasis to certain parts of a character According to Tinker (ibid: 1963: 42) this mix of thick and thin strokes helps us to identify characters more easily.

A serif font (Times New Roman)

A sans serif font (Arial)

A CAPS ONLY DECORATIVE FONT (JUDAS)

A traditional font (Black chancery)

A handwriting font (comic sans)

A shadow font (Shadow)

A script-style font (Ariston)

A fun font – Bucaneer

A delicate, elegant font (Bodoni)

Figure 8.8 There are thousands of fonts

So why use sans serif? Although sans serif fonts are probably not so legible when grouped together in words, they are more perceptible as characters. They catch the eye better from a distance and can be more easily distinguished from further away. Sans serif fonts are always a popular choice for advertising hoardings or road signs. However, although they are more perceptible and are easier to distinguish at a distance or in difficult circumstances, they are not so easy to read in a block. It is as though we can identify each letter more easily, but have to read them individually, while a serif font allows us to read a whole word, or even several words, at once. Because of this effect, reading a block of type in a serif font is much easier. We can read more and read more quickly in a serif font. For these reasons, newspapers and magazines often use serif fonts for body text and sans serif fonts for headlines. The easy-to-see headlines grab your attention, even from a distance, but the serif text is then easy and efficient to read.

The difference is like switching between shouting and talking. Shouting may well catch the attention and allow you to absorb short sentences quickly, but it very soon becomes wearing if someone is shouting at you all the time. The subtleties of the normal conversational voice are much more expressive for long periods of conversation.

It is no surprise that the optician's test card aims for perceptibility and is set in sans serif, while most books go for legibility and serifs.

Font styles and the iconic appeal of type

According to Tinker, most seriffed fonts read as easily as each other (ibid.). Yet there are hundreds of different typefaces available to the designer. Why is this, and why use one rather than another?

Most newspapers and magazines will try to keep to a handful of fonts for everyday use. This makes the newspaper easy to identify because readers become used to the look of certain fonts. Pages look much neater and are easier to read if there are only a limited number of different fonts on a page. However, every newspaper or magazine will occasionally use a decorative or unusual font to say something out the ordinary. Figure 8.9 shows how different fonts can be used to add an extra dimension to the message contained in the actual words used.

Display fonts of this sort should be used sparingly but in the right circumstances they can really add to the message being conveyed.

Displaying and using type

Within any font, there are a number of ways the face can be displayed to make it look different while maintaining the continuity of using the same font. These

Sign up for a brand new life

The handwriting-style font helps make this headline personal.

all the luck of the irish

The typically Irish font emphasises the Irish element of the story.

STAY SNUG WITH YOUR GAS BOILER

The headline says: stay snug. The font emphasises the cold.

Figure 8.9   Different fonts

differences include using condensed, bold, italic, extended, bold italic or bold condensed type and so on.

Using the same font but in these different formats gives the designer a wide range of materials. Bold and italic can be used to add emphasis to a word or paragraph. Bold type is much more legible than roman type, while italic type (according to Tinker (1963)) is far less easy to read.

Bold faces look like this.

Italic faces look like this.

An extended or condensed face changes the *set* of the type. The set is the width of individual characters. In the days of cast type, a foundry would produce condensed or extended faces, but these would normally only be bought by a newspaper in one size, so an editor would talk about it as though it were a different font – Helios bold condensed, for instance. But with computers, it is now easy to set a font not only to any size, but also to any set width and so to produce a Helios bold in 127 point and a set width of so many points (or say 90 per cent) is easy.

Adding extra definition to the font such as bold, italic, shadow, outline is also easy, often as easy as a keystroke on the computer. But one should avoid putting in a different emphasis just because you can. There needs to be a good reason for it.

Another major consideration is whether to set in upper case or lower case. Capital letters are sometimes called upper case because in the old days of hand setting of cast type, the boxes carrying the capital letters were in a case physically above those carrying the lower case letters. Tinker (1963: 57) cites Starch as reporting that lower case letters are read 10 per cent faster than capital letters. Readers also preferred lower case by 90:10. Tinker himself found even more startling figures, reporting that students read lower case 14 per cent faster (ibid.). He identified the shape of the words as one reason for this effect. In lower case most words have a much more clearly identifiable shape than in upper case (see Figure 8.10).

Figure 8.10 Not only do capital letters take up more space, but they are also less easy to read. The lower case word forms an easy-to-recognise shape, while the capital letters are just a block

STRUCTURING TEXT

The space around paragraphs and the space around words is as important as the space around individual characters. Paragraphs of type can be displayed in four main ways:

- The right-aligned paragraph, sometimes called ragged left.

- The left-aligned paragraph, sometimes called ragged right.

- The centre-aligned paragraph, sometimes called ragged both.

- And finally the justified paragraph (see Figure 8.11).

Figure 8.11 Top left: text is ranged left. Top right: text is ranged right. Bottom left: text is centred. Bottom right: text is justified

The justified paragraph requires the copy to have been hyphenated so that long words are not unduly squeezed trying to fit within a line. This can be a particular problem on the narrow column widths favoured by tabloid newspapers.

Newspapers use columns because they aid readability. A column width of 10 ems (almost four centimetres) is fairly normal although quality papers sometimes have slightly wider columns while tabloid columns can be as narrow as 8 ems.

The optimum is said to be 15 ems. A column wider than this becomes difficult to read as the eye has to scan the line in several jumps. Giles and Hodgson (1996: 137) say that a column width should be chosen with an eye to the paper's readership. This makes sense. An educated readership that can read quickly and efficiently will want a longer line so that they can read more in one go. A less well educated readership, for whom reading is more of a chore may find a narrower column width more acceptable.

The proportions of a character in any typeface are vital. The ideal character needs to be oblong rather than square. If the x-height is too large, the all-important ascenders and descenders become indistinguishable, making reading difficult. On the other hand, a large x-height makes the type appear larger and therefore easier to read and it also means fewer words per sentence.

A serif is the curly part of type that hangs off the ends. It adds definition to ascenders and descenders making reading much easier. Since the ascenders and descenders are vital to our ability to read quickly this is important and could be the reason why serif faces are more readable.

Type has a lot of work to do. It must allow the reader to pick up the words as quickly and as easily as possible without using up too much space. To do this, a face must be relatively small, but still be perfectly readable. The amount of space for each character also affects the speed and ease with which type is read. Too much white space around a character makes it as difficult to read as too little. Space between paragraphs breaks the text into bite-sized chunks. The same kind of space between lines makes the whole thing too difficult to read. Too little space and the words become cramped, crushing in on each other. You need to give considerable thought to the type and spacing you use for any publication.

DEVICES TO ADD INTEREST

There are a wide range of devices which can be used to improve the look and readability of a page or which add emphasis or urgency.

Drop letters. These are probably one of the earliest ways of providing an entry point. Monastic scripts used to be big on highly decorated and illuminated drop letters. It left the reader in no doubt about where to start reading. Modern drop letters, used judiciously throughout a piece of text can keep it interesting, prevent it looking too grey and allow the reader to absorb the piece in reasonably easy-to-read segments.

Indented text. Another way to add emphasis or change the pace of a piece of text is to indent it. Indenting the first line by an em space gives a clear indication of where each paragraph starts. It allows the reader to quickly find their way back into the column of text and is a useful guide. Paragraph indents are not essential, but they are helpful to the reader. A hanging indent is the opposite of standard paragraph indenting. Here the first line is run full out and the rest of the paragraph is indented, usually by an em space. This allows the text to stand away from the text in the left-hand column, giving plenty of white space and definition. It is a technique that is useful for extended captions or *sidebar* stories.

It is also possible to indent individual paragraphs. 'Full out' text runs right across the column leaving only a little space before the next column. By indenting, you can increase the space and so, by increasing the white space, highlight that paragraph pulling it away from the rest of the text. You can indent both sides or only one. Generally speaking, indenting both sides is more pleasing unless you intend using vertical scoring (see below) or the text runs alongside a picture or graphic.

Boxed text. If you want to box a piece of copy, you will have to indent both sides in order to give space for the box. Boxes give very definite emphasis and are useful for small stories that are worth more than their size would suggest. They are also good for sidebar stories – additions to a main story that are not too long but are deserving of more emphasis. Boxes can be complete, open (top, bottom or one side), shadowed or on tone and come in a variety of rule size. An open box is useful if you wish to tie in the boxed story with something else: you can put the open side alongside the tied-in story. Rules greater than 6pt would be extremely unusual and tend to look too heavy.

Boxes can also be produced by reversing the copy or laying it on tone (either black on tone or white on tone) or by underlying with colour. All of these devices make the text more difficult to read and so you should also consider using an increase in type size. It is also wise to only use these techniques for short stories.

Bold text. Emboldening text adds emphasis. A short story tied in with others or one you wish to lift from the page can be emboldened. This often works well with a light headline. Emboldening paragraphs within a story helps break up a long story and adds emphasis. You can even embolden a single word for emphasis.

Italic text. Italic text manages to add an ingredient of urgency to text. Italic can be used for emphasis but is better used where you want to introduce an element of breathlessness. Long pieces of italic (anything over thirty words) are very difficult to read, but short phrases or paragraphs can add real importance to the words. It is very useful in *blurbs*.

Underlined text. This also adds emphasis but is slightly self-important and not very fashionable. It is reminiscent of the slightly potty letter writer who writes on lined paper in green ink with a mix of caps and lower case underlining every third word. Still, underlined text is useful in small doses, and invariably with bold text.

Caps. Putting the occasional paragraph in caps (especially small caps) can add further emphasis. I would always use this with bold text to double the impact. Like underlining, it is somewhat unfashionable.

Font breakers. Using a different font can be very dramatic adding a lot of emphasis. Although sans serif faces are less readable because of their high perceptibility, a small paragraph of emboldened sans serif in a long run of text can really draw the eye, encouraging the reader to keep at it.

Staggered font size. Entry points can be emphasised with an increase in typeface. Increasing typefaces for intros can emphasise the entry point and some papers use sizeable emboldened sans serif faces for their lead story intros because they are highly legible and mean the reader should have found the entry point and read the intro before they are really aware of it.

Vertical scoring. This ties in well with indents, especially when the indent is on one side only. The score fills in the indent so that the column sides are even but the rule (from 6 to 18pt) adds heavy emphasis to the paragraph (see Figure 8.12).

Bulleted text. Bullets are also known as blobs to give 'blob pars'. These bullets are devices at the beginning of each par. Usually they are round, but they can be any shape: square, asterisk, arrows, triangles, the list is as long as your imagination. They are usually used with indented text to give the impression of a hanging indent. Sometimes they are used like a drop letter and inserted into the first line or lines of the par. Where the bullets are dropped into several lines, they become a very useful device allowing you to use bits of artwork or logos at the beginning of each par. For instance, a column of international nibs could avoid headlines by running the pars close together but with a globe of the world dropped into the first two lines of each par.

Bullet devices are good for:

- lists of items;
- short paragraphs one after the other;
- a short paragraph added at the end of a story that is separate to it but connected.

TWO PEOPLE were killed and four others injured in a multiple pile up on the M62 yesterday.

The accident happened in fog near the Huddersfield turn off. Police believe that one of the drivers may have been distracted by activity at a building close to the motorway.

The two killed were Mr John Bates, of High St, Chorley and Mr Peter Sims of Bassenthwaite Lane, Oldham.

The injured were taken to hospital but were later released. They were said to be suffering from shock and minor cuts and bruises.

A police spokesman said: "Lorries were being loaded under bright lights at factories alongside the motorway and we believe that one of the drivers might have been momentarily distracted. With the fog so thick, a moment is all that it would have taken."

Four cars were involved in the accident and police were surprised that more were not drawn in. The spokesman said: "Luckily, the accident happened in the inside lane and so other drivers were able to

Witnesses

avoid the crash fairly easily. It was also easy for us to remove the cars from the carriageway very quickly."

By JOHN SMITH
TWO PEOPLE were killed and four others injured in a multiple pile up on the M62 yesterday.

The accident happened in fog near the Huddersfield turn off. Police believe that one of the drivers may have been distracted by activity at a building close to the motorway.

The two killed were Mr John Bates, of High St, Chorley and Mr Peter Sims of Bassenthwaite Lane, Oldham.

The injured were taken to hospital but were later released. They were said to be suffering from shock and minor cuts and bruises.

A police spokesman said: "Lorries were being loaded under bright lights at factories alongside the motorway and we believe that one of the drivers might have been momentarily distracted. With the fog so thick, a moment is all that it would have taken."

Four cars were involved in the accident and police were surprised that more were not drawn in. The spokesman said: "Luckily, the accident happened in the inside lane and so other drivers were able to avoid the crash fairly easily. It was also easy for us to remove the cars from the carriageway very quickly."

Police were on the scene in just a few minutes, according to witnesses and were able to prevent any further carnage.

TWO PEOPLE were killed and four others injured in a multiple pile up on the M62 yesterday.

The accident happened in fog near the Huddersfield turn off. Police believe that one of the drivers may have been distracted by activity at a building close to the motorway.

The two killed were Mr John Bates, of High St, Chorley and Mr Peter Sims of Bassenthwaite Lane, Oldham.

The injured were taken to hospital but were later released. They were said to be suffering from shock and minor cuts and bruises.

A police spokesman said: "Lorries were being loaded under bright lights at factories alongside the motorway and we believe that one of the drivers might have been momentarily distracted. With the fog so thick, a moment is all that it would have taken."

Four cars were involved in the accident and police were surprised that more were not drawn in. The spokesman said: "Luckily, the accident happened in the inside lane

Witnesses

and so other drivers were able to avoid the crash fairly easily. It was also easy for us to remove the cars from the carriageway very quickly."

Police were on the scene in just a few minutes, according to witnesses

Figure 8.12 Different ways of breaking a long run of type. Left: an indented, emboldened paragraph and a side-head. Centre: A drop cap in one of the paragraphs. Right: An indented paragraph with a vertical score and a crosshead. These tend to look better in a run of text than a side-head – they tend to give the impression of a new story

Bylines. Bylines – the name of the reporter credited with writing a story – give wide scope for breaking up text. Once only set in bold at the top of the text, they now come in all sizes, with rules or boxes, are added to standfirsts, included with pictures of the reporter – the only limiting factor is your imagination. They can be very useful for breaking up columns of text or placing at the top of a second column of text, underneath a double column intro (see Figure 6.11).

Standfirsts. Standfirsts are a round-up of some major event that explains why the article is there, written in under thirty or even fifteen words in a way that makes a story sound irresistible. They are also a useful way of going over old ground that it would not be wise to take for granted, and are perhaps the ultimate art of a good sub.

Captions. Provided the caption for a picture is easy to find, you have a wide range of opportunities to break up a page with a caption. Different types, rules, reverses etc., are all tricks that can make a page seem more interesting. A drop letter or word and sequential caption can be used here. A feature following the army as they practise for a major campaign for instance may have a number of pictures that could be captioned as: DAY 1: the army sets up camp. DAY 2: and we're ready for manoeuvres. etc.

Rules and borders. Rules and borders can be used to break up stories or to connect and add emphasis. Rules and borders can run into headlines, through, into, under or over pictures and graphics. They come in a variety of sizes, shapes and designs: from the famous dotted rule (as in tear along the dotted line) to fancy borders with a variety of uses from holly borders for Christmas pages to fancy scroll borders. Rules come in sizes from 0.5pt to 24pt. Don't forget that there are tone rules, white rules and all the colours of the rainbow in between.

White space. Careful use of white space adds more emphasis than you would imagine. Compare the white space in the *Guardian* with other papers and see the effect it has.

Crossheads. Crossheads and sideheads are great for breaking up long slabs of text. They can be used in a wide variety of ways but should be kept to the same style throughout a page. You can have fun with the crossheads, linking them together throughout the text by providing a running theme. However, you do need to be careful you don't spell out a message you didn't mean to. One sub's final message to the boss after his acrimonious departure was spelt out in the initial letters of crossheads throughout the lead item.

Devices should be used sparingly and with coherence. Too many differing devices will make a page just as unreadable as a page which is just one big slab of text.

9
Words in type

Although the choice of type used to set words is critical, so is the choice of the words themselves. The whole point of design is to sell the journalism contained on the printed pages and it has been assumed throughout this book that the copy to be used is well-written and well-edited. I have relied on other books to discuss how to get these vital tasks right. But there are other writing and editing tasks required as part of the design process and it is important to know how to do these in order to produce a lively and attractive page.

WRITING HEADLINES

A headline is there to sell the story below it.

As we have discussed before, readers leaf through a publication looking for something to grab their attention – an entry point to draw them into a page. A good headline attracts attention and should make the reader want to read the story. A good headline should make the story sound like just what they would want to read. This means that the headline should be aimed at the target audience: if you are writing a headline for the *Sun* or *Loaded*, there is not much point in writing a serious-minded headline or one that contains clever literary allusions, the reader will either be uninterested or will miss the point. The headline should contain cultural references that your readers will understand and want to relate to, it should excite them about a story that they will want to read.

The headline should tell the reader a little bit about the story – but not enough to let them think they know all about it and no longer need to read it! A heading or headline aimed at a young audience hooked on *Big Brother* might say:

Big Brother's June dishes
dirt on house sex romps

There are key words that are going to draw in the readers: 'Sex romps', is an obvious phrase to draw attention as is 'dishes dirt'. *Big Brother* drew thousands of readers to magazines and newspapers in the 15–25 age group, so it is a good phrase to use in a heading. However the headline does not go into detail. If the reader wants to know the 'dirt' and learn about the 'sex romps' he or she is going to have to read the article – and there is barely a *Big Brother* fan alive who could resist that one!

Headlines need to be active. They should be in the present or future tense in order to keep them immediate and urgent. It also makes them shorter and simpler to read. By saying that June 'dishes dirt' (present tense) the headline is active and suggests that this 'dishing dirt' is a continuing process and one that is new and up to date. Although the interview must have taken place at least the day before, probably much longer ago if this was in a magazine, the present tense keeps it live and current.

Headlines must be sentences and should always contain a verb to provide action: June 'dishes' dirt. This verb is carefully chosen to give the correct balance of action combined with colloquial usage. It implies more than a verb such as 'telling' could, it suggest the narrator will get to the nitty gritty, the material you really want to hear about without equivocating or dressing it up in prissy language. Of course whether the story actually goes into the depth of detail the reader is hoping for is another matter, but if the headline implies it, then the reader will soon get stuck in. Your choice of verbs in the story text is also vital, of course, but it is especially so in headlines because you rarely have room for adverbs or adjectives and so the correct choice of verb and noun is vital. 'Britney storms out' is much more expressive than 'Well-known singer walks out in a bit of a huff' even if we don't know where or what she walked out of.

You should avoid putting your opinions into headlines; they should explain the story, not your view of it. This means that there are words of which you need to be careful. For instance, the phrase hard-left politician (or hard-right) is widely used in a disparaging way. But there is no easy definition of what is hard-left or hard-right, they are relative descriptions that are used to disparage someone's political viewpoint in an attempt to dismiss it without proper thought. If the term is used by a politician about someone, then you could use it, but it is not a term you should use for your own description. A headline needs to be accurate and should avoid straying from the facts presented in the copy. The Press Complaints Commission (PCC) is as likely to uphold a complaint against a newspaper for an inaccurate headline as for inaccurate text. Jonathan Aitken – a former MP – complained against the *Observer* in 1993 about the headline 'Aitken named in arms bribe case' saying that it incorrectly implied that he was involved in wrongdoing. The PCC accepted that: '. . . the text of the story did give details of the extent of the complainant's involvement which made it clear that he was not 'named' in any sense of being involved with wrongdoing in the arms bribe case or evasion of US export controls' (PCC Report 16 1993: 8).

Journalistic jargon or clichés are another trap for the eager sub-editor. It is tempting to use journalese such as 'bid', 'blaze', 'slash', 'rap', or 'quiz' because all the papers seem to. This is sloppy writing and should be avoided. Fresh headings are bound to seem more attractive than jargoned headings such as 'Bravery bid in fire dash'. To show you how weak cliché headings can be, try the headline generator (Figure 9.1). Choose one word from each column and see what you get. There is no need to follow the horizontal lines, but you can only choose one word out of each column in that order. Some make more sense than others, but all work, more or less, and rely heavily on cliché.

1	2	3	4	5
Disgraced	Hero	raps	babyfaced	love-cheat
Brave	Mum	accuses	royal	baby
Sad	schoolkid	praises	disgraced	boyfriend
Have-a-go	Mr Chips	angers	sexy	girlfriend
Happy	copper	burns	kinky	lads
Missing	cult	serenades	illegal	girls
Crazy	star	bedded	legit	son
Soccer	sex-pest	slaps	sweet	daughter
Disgraced	worker	shoots	sour	wife
Defiant	woman	saves	cruel	hubby
Disabled	Mrs mop	slams	gorgeous	blackmailer
Drunken	Dad	wins	obsessed	fortune
Sexy	stepmum	fights	rip-off	cash
Mystery	pensioner	hurt in	raging	child
Wicked	thug	rescues	dead	star
Wild	rocker	fires	angry	celeb
Depraved	athlete	sacks	old	Scrooge
Hairy	student	stabs	new	animal
Tubby	granny	bags	broken	babe
Skinny	DJ	babies	bitter	hunk
Racist	yuppie	quits	slighted	maniac
Cruel	hubby	steals	shamed	killer
Barmy	wife	loses	shattered	thief

Figure 9.1 A cliché-headline generator

There is also jargon that comes from other sources and specialist words that are not in common usage. These might come from politicians, showbiz stars, scientists or technicians. We should avoid using them if it is unlikely that readers will understand them. Of course, if you are working for *New Scientist*, then a reasonable smattering of widely-used scientific terms would be acceptable in headlines and it would probably be difficult to write without them. Similarly, writing for financial publications introduces a specialist vocabulary that would need to be used. But try to avoid phrases or words with which the target audience of your publication will be unfamiliar. Acronyms or abbreviations are also potential trouble. 'PCC' might mean Press Complaints Commission to readers of *Press Gazette*, but to the purchasers of *The Church Times* it would be Parochial Church Council. If you are sure your readership understands the abbreviation, that there is only one interpretation and the abbreviation is widely used, then by all means put it in the headline. For instance, 'Aids' is probably more widely understood now than Acquired Immune Deficiency Syndrome, and readers would certainly take longer to remember what the British Broadcasting Corporation is than good old 'BBC' or even 'The Beeb'.

A headline must make sense and it should also make sense line by line – or at least not imply something you did not mean. A famous wartime headline read:

French push bottles
up Germans rear

(or so Sellers claims (1968a: 98)). Read as a single line, this makes better sense:

French push bottles up German rear

Read a headline out loud – are there hidden meanings? Does slang turn it into something that will be sniggered at? Good editors have dirty minds and a wide appreciation of slang both obscene and regional. They need it to avoid headlines such as:

Jilted lover
loosened
boyfriend's nuts

which was written by a sub about a court case concerning a man who tried to scare off a rival by loosening the wheel nuts on his car. Another example concerns a TV advertising campaign against pickpockets based around the slogan 'snatch of the week'. This came to an abrupt end a few years ago, presumably after someone pointed out that Midlands slang made this advert 'snigger of the week' in some parts of the country where 'snatch' meant something very different.

A headline must fit the space available for it. These days you will usually be writing the heading direct onto the computer screen and you will be able to see whether the chosen type size 'busts' (is too long) the headline or leaves it 'shy' (too short).

Where the headline is not being set directly on the page, but you are writing it to be set by someone else, it is even more important to ensure that it will fit in the space available. Traditionally this is done by using type tables showing how many characters at a certain size of font would fit into the space available. For instance, working in Helvetica bold, at 60pt you might find that across 53 ems, you could have a character count of 18. You would then need to count the number of characters in your headline. This is done by counting each lower case character as one or each capital letter as one and a half. Some letters differ and 'w' and 'm' should be counted as one and a half in lower case or two in capitals, and the characters 'I', 'J', 'F' and 'T' should be counted as half in lower case and one in capitals. If, when using a computer page make-up system, the headline doesn't quite fit, it can be tempting to adjust a headline's size, especially if the headline is a good one. There is usually no reason why you can't reduce say, a 60pt headline to 58pt in order to make it fit, but you should be careful about adjusting the word spacing or set as this effects the look of the font. Some editorial offices do not allow subs to reduce type to arbitrary numbers, although I've never understood why. In hot metal days, type was adjusted in 12pt steps, because it was impossibly expensive to carry a full range of sizes. Consequently one had 30pt, 36pt, 48pt, 60pt and 72pt. But now that we can use any size, I can see no reason not to use the range on offer provided the balance of heading size is right for the page.

The shape of a headline is also important (see Figure 9.2). The balance between different lines of heading in a multi-line heading will effect how the page looks. If there are only two lines, then they should both fill the space fairly well and certainly should not be more than one column shy. Both lines should be of similar length. Three-lined headings, should tend to have the middle line smaller than the other two as this looks more balanced; the same applies to multi-lined headings.

With multi-heading display, always write the main heading first so that it can tell the story with any straplines or subsidiary headings written later. Make sure you do not repeat the same word in any of the other headings and avoid punctuation. If you must put things in quotes, then single quote marks should be used. Normal punctuation rules apply, but you should avoid headlines that need punctuating. Do not put a full point after the heading.

Two killed in M-way pile-up

Drivers die in M-way pile-up

M-way drivers killed

Roadside 'distraction' claims two

Figure 9.2 Top: a two-line heading. Both lines need to be about the same length and certainly should not be more than one column shorter than the other.

Centre: Four lines. The top and bottom lines need to be the longest of the four and should be of similar length.

Bottom: A two-deck headline. The second deck should be about half the typesize of the first deck. Try to keep the lines of the second deck of equal length

Normal rules about capital letters apply, so do not use cap starts for words unless they are proper nouns or the first word of a sentence. Check finally that the heading fits, has no double meaning, is legally safe and makes sense.

The heading must come first on any page and if this means re-writing the intro after the heading has been finished then this will have to be done. Often the obvious heading is in the intro or sounds very similar and so the intro needs to be rewritten to avoid repetition.

DIFFERENT STYLES OF HEADING

The several different types of heading have their own particular names and uses but all are there to allow the designer to prevent the text running through from one heading to the next.

Kickers

Kickers use a completely different style of font in order to give a story a particular emphasis. This is the same kind of emphasis that TV tries to inject with the 'And finally . . .' news item. You should only use one kicker font per page, allowing a particular story to stand away from the rest, giving it a distinctiveness even though its heading style and content do not make it the top story on the page. Often the kicker font will be sans serif when the usual font is serif, or vice versa. The *Sun* used to use Cooper Black as its kicker, a bold font with heavy, stylised serifs that stood up well against heavy sans serif fonts used throughout the rest of the page.

Multi-column headings

Single column headings carry little weight and are generally used to introduce small down page stories. However, they can be inserted within a block of text either to split it or to add emphasis either as a heading or as a device to carry a strong quote or reinforce a part of the story. Nowadays most headings cover several columns from the down page double column to the multi-column lead heading. The broader the heading, the stronger the display and the more material required as support beneath the heading.

Multi-line headings

There is no real limit to the number of lines a heading can be, although it is rare to see one deeper than six lines and most are between two and four. The more lines there are, the narrower the heading will normally be. A full-page streamer dropping down four lines would look extremely odd and over-heavy no matter how important the story. On the other hand, a single line streamer will probably require an additional heading to give the appropriate emphasis. Generally we can say that the average lead headline fills 10–12 column widths. The average second lead heading would probably fill 6–10 column widths.

Writing standfirsts and bylines

There are a variety of text devices used on pages by designers to assist the reader to navigate the page and attract the reader into a story. Standfirsts are the first device usually used. This is a cross between a headline and the intro to the story, it often also combines a byline – the name of the story's author. The standfirst is more likely to be used on a longer story, probably a feature or news backgrounder. It is particularly important in magazines.

A standfirst is usually presented in a font size that is larger than the story text, but much smaller than the headline. Anything from 14pt to 30pt could be considered normal, although a larger font is possible. It is possible to use much more detail in a standfirst than in a headline and it will often contain one of the more interesting anecdotes used within the story (see Figure 9.3). So a story about how a celebrity overcame their drug addiction might have a headline such as 'My heroin hell' followed by a standfirst that said: 'My family had left me, my life was a mess. I had lost my job and I lived in squalor. What had happened to my golden life as TV's soap queen? *Spenders* star Jane Zilfur talks to Chris Frost about celebrity, fame and drugs.'

This relatively short but easy to spot entry point gives readers key elements that allows them to decide whether or not they want to read the story, although of course if the designer and editor have done their job properly, the reader will hardly be able to resist.

If a standfirst is used, then the traditional intro (probably the one that the reporter had written) needs to be changed otherwise it is likely to conflict with the standfirst. The editor needs to ensure that the headline, the standfirst and the intro fit together as a whole.

Standfirsts often contain bylines and sometimes *picture bylines* (see Figure 9.3). Bylines are seen as a reward for good work by most journalists and getting a byline is still considered important. However, it is now unusual to find un-bylined stories in magazines and even in newspapers; if the story is of any length, a byline is normal. If the byline is not included in a standfirst (or there is no standfirst) then a byline might be included at the front of the text, or even in the text. If it is at the start of the text, it might be just a straight 'By Chris Frost' in a bold version of the body text, or it could be a more detailed description: 'Special

Driving oul lethal loung

Today's roads are busier than ever whilst our cars are more comfortable. JOHN SMITH wonders if they are too relaxing for our own safety and whether we should go back to the hard times of yore.

Lethal comfc

Today's roads are busier than ever whilst our cars are more comfortable. Motoring correspondent CHRIS FROST wonders if they are too relaxing for our own safety.

Figure 9.3   A byline standfirst and picture byline standfirst

report by Chris Frost, Education correspondent', 'An exclusive report by . . .'
(see Figure 9.4). If the name is to be included in the text (and this really is a
style issue – how does your publication do these things?) then it might have
'. . . writes Chris Frost' at the end of the intro paragraph.

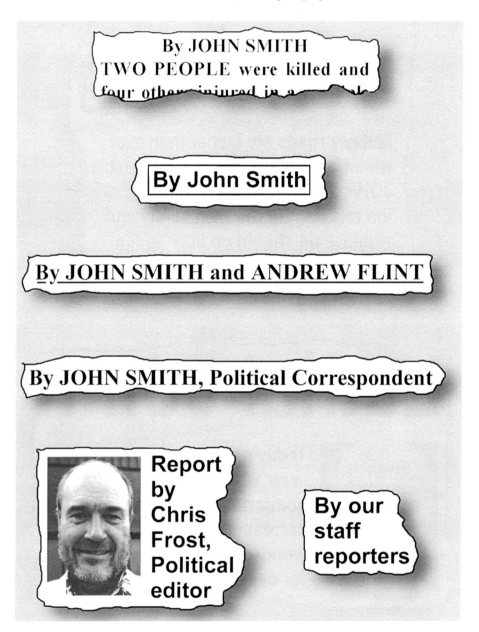

Figure 9.4 A variety of byline styles

CAPTIONS

The caption is another text device that needs to stand out from the general run of text. This can be achieved either by making it slightly larger or putting it in bold, italic or a different font. Italic can add emphasis but has been out of fashion for some time now. This must partly be because it is difficult to read, but also because it appears fussy and old-fashioned. No doubt it will become fashionable in some retro move, but probably not for a while. By setting the caption in a sans serif face against a seriffed body text, particularly if it is emboldened, the caption stands away from the body text and there can be no confusion about it being read in with the text.

Captions are usually provided with pictures or graphics to explain details within the picture (see Figure 9.5 on page 114 for caption ideas). If you need a caption to explain a picture then maybe it would be better not to use the picture, so do consider carefully what goes in the caption. If there are people, objects or places that need description then this should be done. The usual format for a photo of people is to put: 'pictured from left to right are: xxxxx'. It is worth remembering that while sub-editors sometimes get bored and like to put captions in odd places: up the sides of the picture, within the border, hidden in a section of the picture or in another column, readers never get bored with having captions in an obvious place where they can find them easily. If someone wants to know the name of the person in the picture, they don't like searching for captions and we should make them easily available.

A caption is there to help the reader make sense of the picture and if it requires too much explanation, it's worth considering whether to use the picture at all. As discussed in the next chapter, a picture should be capable of telling the story and the caption should only be there to fill in the details, usually explaining who is in the picture. A caption should be adding to the picture, not saying the same thing. It can offer detail, or describe what happened before or what is about to happen. We should be confident that the picture and caption tell the whole story.

Figure 9.5 (overleaf)   A variety of caption styles

LEFT: The town centre that will have to be demolished to make way for the new motorway. Protestors are set to blockade the centre from Saturday.

The town centre that will have to be demolished to make way for the new motorway.

Due for demolition to make way for a new motorway.

Due for demolition to make way for a new motorway.

10
Using pictures

Pictures are one of the key elements of a page. It is pictures that draw a reader into a page and help to guide him or her through the page and the material on it. This means that considerable care needs to be taken in the choice of pictures and how they are used.

'A picture's worth a thousand words' is an oft-used phrase, but one that has the wrong emphasis. In publication terms it must be turned on its head, a picture must be worth its space in words before we can consider using it.

This often becomes difficult in a local paper, trade journal or in-house publication. A national newspaper or magazine has at its disposal dozens of top photographers desperate to illustrate all the really good stories – and has the budget to pay for them.

But a small publication may have to rely solely on freelance photographers who are constantly asked to cover boring, but difficult-to-get-out-of presentations, awards and retirements. A good photographer who makes these bread and butter pictures exciting, original and worthy of publication is rare and well worth a good salary. Unfortunately he or she rarely gets it – at least on the publication that they start working for.

You may also be forced to take your own pictures. Digital cameras, with their direct links to computers make this job easier technically but still difficult creatively. The National Union of Journalists has traditionally opposed this practice for the very good reason that good writers don't often make good photographers and vice versa because no-one has the time to do both jobs well. However, employers are often keen that reporters should take photographs and it is certainly right that good reporters should be aware of the importance of good images to go with text. There is a big difference between knowing what makes a good picture and having the time and talent to take one. Having said that, good reporters should always carry a cheap camera, even if it's only a disposable instant camera, in case something dramatic happens. The poor quality of some of the early video of the September 11 disaster did not prevent it being used because it was all there was. Better to get a poor picture than no picture at all.

Editors also find that they are often pressured by an advertiser or good contact to produce or use boring pictures of award ceremonies or products. There is also the view, still widely held on local papers, that faces sell papers. A group shot of thirty local people in a picture will sell thirty papers, so the wisdom goes. I can't help thinking that people are a little more sophisticated these days. Those thirty might well buy the paper, but another eighty might cancel their subscription because they are fed up with boring photographs of groups of people.

It is also the case that this continual exposure to boring pictures makes it difficult for the editor choosing or editing pictures to make the best use of something different when it does come along. It is all too easy to think of pictures merely as three- or four-column space fillers. It is always important to examine each picture as it is presented and decide whether or not to use it on its merits. A good picture uses the space allotted to it in the best way possible. A good picture should:

1.   Illustrate and illuminate quickly and effectively what the story is all about.

2.   Underline the emotive side of the story.

3.   Hint at action.

4.   Allow the reader to identify with the people in the story.

It may well be that one picture can do all these things, but these pictures are rare. Usually more than one picture is needed to describe the full spread of a story.

It is up to the editor to decide whether one picture is used to illustrate one aspect of a story, or whether more than one is used. The decision will depend on the story, the pictures and the space available.

MAKING A POINT

Pictures can be used to ram home a point made in the page display. If the picture is worth that magic thousand words, then use it. Nothing makes the point about the carnage and waste of life in the latest war or terrorist outrage than a picture of the dead and dying; nothing sums up the triumph of a World Cup victory better than a jubilant captain carried shoulder high waving the trophy at the team's supporters.

Picture selection is a difficult and subjective task. Explaining why a picture works with a particular story is complex. Any picture that is worth its place on a newspaper page must be paying its way with added information for the reader. It must help us describe what is going on. An aerial picture of the site of an incident can help readers picture the place, particularly if it is a rural area where immediate identification is difficult, unlike towns where an address will often suffice. But even here, a map and picture of the premises can often make things clearer. Pictures of objects can aid identification.

An archaeological find, for instance, can be pictured much more easily and to better effect than by description. People too can be better served by pictures. A description of the bouncy and hirsute David Bellamy will never call him to mind as well and as quickly as a picture.

Similarly, no amount of cunningly-crafted prose is going to say as much about the courage of Falklands war veteran Simon Weston as a picture of his face complete with its unnaturally tight skin grafts crisscrossing the few remaining tufts of hair left on his head. One picture of this man sat comfortably at ease with his disfigurement says more about his courage and ability to come to terms with his fate than any amount of writing could.

Pictures have a major part to play in setting the emotional agenda of a piece. Whether they are pictures of widows weeping at a pithead mining disaster or the triumphant smile of the sports victor or the mouth-twisting absorption of a picture-painting toddler, they all add something to the reader's perception of what has happened.

Choosing pictures to go with stories and features becomes a way of emphasising and underlining the areas of the story that are strongest. Harold Evans believes there are three tests for a publishable picture and that a picture without any of them 'should be rejected as junk'. The three tests are:

1. Animation

2. Relevant context

3. Depth of meaning
                    (Evans 1978: 47)

Evans is not suggesting that you must have all three at once, although a picture that did could well be a winner. Animation gives activity and a lively picture that invites the reader to discover more, although Evans makes it clear that by animation he doesn't mean activity but life: 'a set scowl or a closed eye may give animation to a picture' (Evans 1978: 69). Relevant context helps to explain what is going on or adds extra information and so supports the story, while depth of meaning also supports the story adding more information but also bringing in the emotional element, to help us feel more about the story.

You should never use a picture with a story just because you have got one. Only if the picture adds to the story should you consider using it. Does the picture add to our understanding of what is happening? Does it help to emphasise what has happened? Does it add to our feeling of identification?

Take the example of the murder of a child. We will certainly want a picture that will show the murder spot, be it a house or a trampled piece of field. This allows people to firmly fix in their mind where the incident took place – either as a place they know or know of or at least as the type of place. They probably know of somewhere similar in their own locality.

The Mainwaring murders in which a father and daughter were killed and their bodies dismembered and left in the garden were covered by all the popular tabloids with a huge aerial picture of the modest semi-detached home with its suburban garden on the front pages. Millions of readers had similar homes – the Mainwarings, the picture confirmed, were just ordinary people like you and me.

A picture of the victim and if possible, the nearest relative will also be required. This is particularly important for local papers where many readers might recognise the picture. But it is also important for national papers where the picture allows us to relate to the victim. It could have been us, or our child, or our mother. Since these pictures are often snapshots from the family album, the pictures show the victim smiling or laughing incongruously. This can add to the poignancy of the story by confirming that the victim is a real person enjoying the same things as the readers. Pictures of murder weapons, the police scurrying back and forth can also add context and animation.

Following an arrest, you would of course want pictures of the accused together with anything that would bring him/her to the reader as a real person and not some shadowy maniac.

Whether a news picture shows someone making a pot from clay; a tearful mother hugging her kidnapped child or a photo of the Ruben's picture that has just sold for a record fifty million pounds it is bound to say more about the event than even the best-written piece could manage. But a picture of twenty safety officers receiving their certificates from their employer probably adds nothing to the story and will require a large amount of space that could be better used for something else. However, an animated demonstration of how they won their certificates might well provide a strong focal point for the page.

Occasionally you will get a picture so good that it requires a different slant than that suggested by the copy. If so, don't be afraid to follow this line. Really good pictures have a massive impact and sometimes the copy must play second fiddle to this. This is why TV quickly became the dominant medium for news.

Shape

One of the first decisions to be made about a picture is what should actually be in it and what shape it should be. The photographer decides what will be in the picture for a variety of reasons – news value, artistic merit, colour and shape, for instance. The editor needs to decide what should be in the picture on the basis of the story and the rest of the page. Not only will the editor need to consider the content of the picture but will also need to consider the shape. Some shapes work better than others in a newspaper or magazine. Changing the shape of a picture can often dramatically influence the way the picture looks and therefore how the story is presented and ultimately how the page is shaped (see Figure 10.1).

A tall picture can look dramatic because it presents us with a view that is different to the normal one. Our eyes allow us to see in landscape; we have a very broad view spanning almost 180 degrees in a horizontal form. But our brow prevents us from seeing too high, presumably on the basis that there's not much up there to see apart from sky and the sun, which is more likely to blind us. A picture that is long rather than wide is therefore unusual and likely to appear dramatic. That doesn't mean a wide picture is wasted however. Often cutting a horizontal picture into a vertically shaped frame would mean missing out a lot of the information we want to include – for exactly the reasons I've just explained.

Be careful not to cut out a picture's setting. A face could have been photographed anywhere. To cut out the part of the picture showing the gas chamber in which a convicted murderer was about to be executed is to waste the picture. Even white space around a picture can add emphasis, particularly if the subject is looking out of the side of the picture.

The shape of a picture can add a lot to the way both the picture and the page look. An unusual shape can add drama and interest to a page. This could be as easy as making it very wide or very tall, but it could involve shaping the edge of a picture in an unusual way with the type so that the type wraps around the picture, emphasising certain attributes.

Square is the most boring shape. A square picture can be a good picture but it struggles to make the best of itself within an all too symmetrical frame. Although a picture will attract attention on the page (as any picture does, according to Garcia and Stark 1991) it will not give the feeling of drama or interest that an unusually shaped picture, or block of pictures will do. This is something of which the entertainment industry is well aware. They know they can add dynamism to their movie products just by producing them on a wide screen. TV is aware of this dimension as well. The new wave of TVs are all wide screen. Even your holiday snaps come on oblong sized paper in order to add impact.

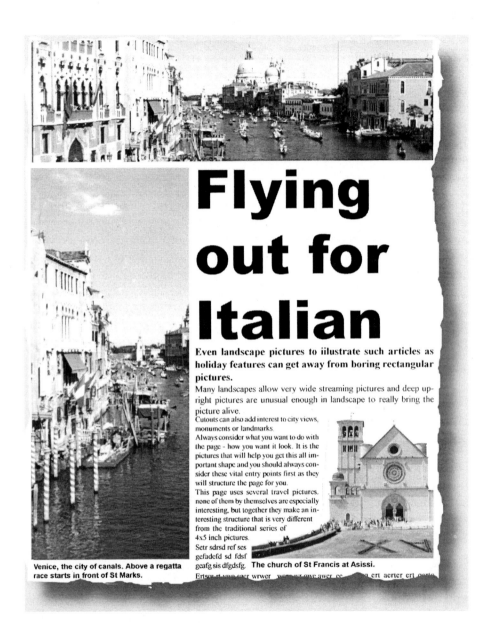

Venice, the city of canals. Above a regatta
race starts in front of St Marks.

The church of St Francis at Asissi.

Figure 10.1a The pictures you choose for a page need to be the best pictures and in the most interesting shapes

Town centre in car park battle

A car park is set to be built across the centre of a landmark town centre.

This type of picture allows the shape of the buildings to be used to break up the normal rectangular shape of a picture. Rather than cut out part of the picture, the much lighter left hand side can sit behind the double column text of the intro. This type of setting requires care as the picture may make the text much less legible. You should keep text off dark areas and use in a slightly larger size, but it does allow for different shapes of picture. In this example, the text is wrapped into the picture, but it would be possible to just lay it over the top, if the background were not too dark.

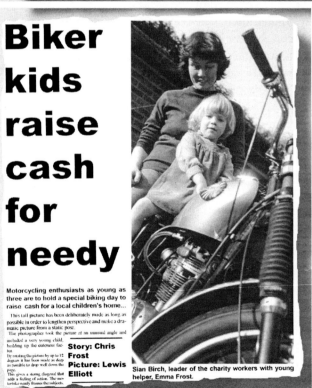

Biker kids raise cash for needy

Motorcycling enthusiasts as young as three are to hold a special biking day to raise cash for a local children's home...

This tall picture has been deliberately made as long as possible in order to lengthen perspective and make a dramatic picture from a static pose.

The photographer took the picture at an unusual angle and included a very young child, building up the cuteness factor.

By rotating the picture by up to 12 degrees it has been made as deep as possible to drop well down the page.

This gives a strong diagonal that adds a feeling of action. The motorbike neatly frames the subjects.

Story: Chris Frost
Picture: Lewis Elliott

Sian Birch, leader of the charity workers with young helper, Emma Frost.

Figure 10.1b Picture shapes play an important role in determining the visual shape of a page. Try to avoid square pictures

Common wisdom has it that a 4:5 ratio is the ideal, but you will find that other ratios can also work well.

A good photographer will provide an editor with a variety of shapes: wide or tall. Study them carefully and decide which adds more impact. Often a wide picture will allow for more action as most action we are interested in tends to be in the horizontal plane.

You can also *pierce* a picture so that text or another picture or graphic, is inserted into the picture. This can also add emphasis. It is worth remembering that picture shape is the overall shape, not just the shape of an individual picture. If you have a block of pictures together, then it is how they work together that is important, not the individual shapes.

Cropping pictures

What a picture frames is of vital importance. Everyone has been at an event when a famous person, or perhaps even someone we know has been centre stage – a concert perhaps or the graduation of a favourite relative. Flashbulbs pop and hundreds of pictures are taken, but we know that when the films are developed there will be a picture of the stadium or graduation hall with the subject of the picture a dark and distant dot in the centre. If we could cut out the bits we don't want – such as the ear of the person in front or the large section of audience, the picture that is left would be perfect. This is the process photographers and editors go through all the time because although photographers try to ensure that they have correctly framed what they think the picture should be, they are not always aware of the angle the editor has decided to take. It is also possible that an archive picture is to be used and this would have been taken for a different purpose altogether. Sometimes, of course, we are obliged to use photographs from amateurs which are not well framed. An early cropping decision can completely change a picture (see Figure 10.2).

The editor then has to decide which section of the picture needs to be produced on the page. It might be that the photographer has taken a group photograph, but we only want to use the two people standing in the centre. We would then crop off the people on either side (see Figure 10.3 for an example).

Zooming in on the action is often a good way to make a picture look more exciting. We are better able to see what is going on and getting in very close makes for an angle that is unusual and adds interest. You need to be careful that you are not cutting out important context. Get in too close and although you'll know what's in the picture, for the reader it will seem to be one of those 'guess the identity' pictures that appear in puzzle magazines where a magnified picture of an everyday object leaves us guessing.

Figure 10.2 Cropping and changing the shape of a picture can make a huge difference to the way it looks on the page. Instead of being just a typical landscape, this travel picture has been cropped upright making the scene appear much more dramatic. The caption and headline have been laid over the sea and sky to maximise the space

Figure 10.3 Just because you have a picture of three people doesn't mean your picture has to include them all. If the story concerns only one of them, edit the others out and if necessary, enlarge the portrait you need

Occasionally there might be unavoidable sections of a picture that are distracting or of no value at all. We then have a choice of either piercing the picture to fill that space with text or another picture or to trim away the background leaving parts of the subject of the picture standing outside of the frame. This is a useful technique. It makes the subject look larger than life and pulls them away from the background. It adds the illusion of depth to the picture and allows you to make the subject of the picture slightly larger than the space actually allowed for the picture. The *Daily Mail* is very fond of this technique and uses it extensively – favouring full-figure portraits which require quite a lot of space if the subject is to be seen at a reasonable size. Cutting away the frame and allowing the figure to stand clear is a good way of coping with the problem of space (see Figure 10.4).

Figure 10.4 Cutting away some of the background has several effects. The image can appear larger and the subjects more active, as though they are climbing out of the picture. The unhelpful, dull background is markedly reduced and becomes much less obtrusive

Diagonals

Diagonals are important to a picture. They add drama and excitement; they suggest movement and action. Imagine a runner on the starting blocks. The body is diagonal across the picture. As the runner sprints away, the diagonal continues with the body thrust forward and the arms and legs adding additional diagonals. The picture conveys action and we want to know why this person is running. If they are wearing sports gear, then it will be clear that they are playing a sport, but the picture will still be dramatic and interesting because it involves action. (see Figure 10.5).

Animation

Too many pictures on newspaper pages tend to be static. TV and film producers found out a long time ago that people prefer to watch action. If action cannot be produced by the plot, then it can be produced by the framing. If two people are talking, the producer might get them to walk so that action is introduced in that way. If they are sitting in armchairs talking, a film producer might use extreme close-ups or cut quickly between the two or use still other devices to make the scene more visually interesting. TV producers find this more difficult to do on some current affairs programmes without making them seem contrived, but even here, attempts are made to liven up things by cutting from close-ups

Figure 10.5 You don't have to have photographs from a premier division football match to fill your publication with lively, action-packed pictures. Both these pictures have strong diagonals that start at the bottom left and finish on the top right. Both tell the story of youth football

to long shots, from one camera to another. Imagine watching question time or the *Parkinson Show* with only one camera placed at a distance so that you could see everything without changing cameras. The picture would soon get boring. Instead the producers use several cameras and although in both *Question Time* or *Parkinson* there are just a series of talking heads, the cameras cut in for close-ups so that we can pick up telling facial expressions, zoom out to show us the audience or change view and direction to give a feeling of pace and action.

We can't provide movement in publication pictures (although websites can use small mpeg clips to provide moving pictures) so we have to make sure that even static portraits of people contain animation by being an unusual shape, taken from an unusual angle, containing gestures or actions or being framed unusually to contain additional information. That's why the traditional budget day picture of the Chancellor of the Exchequer holding up the famous red despatch box used to be so popular; it's a bit clichéd now, but it still provides more interest and information than a mugshot of the Chancellor, that could have been taken anytime. Watch the news when famous people are surrounded by the press – see how the flashbulbs flicker and hear the shutters clash as the star moves his or her head or makes a gesture.

Scaling pictures

One of the first tasks for a page designer is deciding on the size of the main picture that will become the entry point for the reader. The Poynter Institute's Eye-trac research shows that readers are drawn into a page by the picture or pictures (Garcia and Stark 1991). The picture is therefore important to a page design and usually becomes the page's entry point, drawing the reader in and then directing them to the start of the main article. The size of the picture is important in this exercise. If the picture fills the whole page, there will be nothing else on that page, although this could well draw the reader onto the opposite page. This is a lot of space however, and when the copy taster is deciding what should go on a page, it is a juggling act to balance the relative importance of a picture against the copy that is competing for the space.

On the other hand, if a picture is too small then readers will not be drawn to it on the page and will not be able to make out much of the information in the picture. A picture of a single person can normally be used in a smaller size than a picture of a group of people for instance, because in order to be identifiable, the people in the picture need to be of a certain size.

However, we would not put a picture of a person on a page and then use a small size just because it is one person. You need, as always, to consider why the picture is being used and what you hope to say with it. If it is there merely to show what the person looks like, then it only needs to be as big as required for that purpose. If it is there to add drama, context, animation and draw the reader into the page, then it may need to be much bigger (see Figure 10.9 for an example).

Once the size of the picture has been chosen, the picture needs to be *scaled*. Just because the photographer has provided the picture at a certain size, we don't have to use it at that size. We can make it smaller or larger. We can also edit the picture (select the section we want to use) as discussed above and then make it smaller or larger. On an electronic system, it is easy to scale the picture once it has been edited. The picture box is drawn to the correct size and the picture is then imported into that frame. Always remember to ensure that the frame has the same proportions as the picture. If the frame proportions are different, you should never stretch the picture to fit as this is nearly always detectable if it involves shrinking or stretching by more than a small percentage. This means that people can end up looking unusually thin, or – more damagingly – unusually fat. Making a person look fatter than they are is a certain way to be flooded with complaints, quite apart from being a distortion. Always try to ensure that you crop the picture so that the proportions of the picture and the frame are the same. That doesn't mean the picture and the frame need to be the same size – you might be reducing or enlarging the picture – but the proportions need to be the same. If the picture is 20 cm × 24 cm and you are intending to use it at half that size (or a quarter if you are talking area), the frame will need to be 10 cm × 12 cm.

Pictures in hard copy

You might occasionally be presented with a proper photograph to use on a page. In order to ensure that the picture is only scanned in at the maximum resolution required, you can scale and *crop* the picture before scanning. This can be done in the same way as if you were scaling and cropping a picture for processing on a traditional process camera. You can either mark the front of the picture with a wax pencil or draw on the back of the photo. Once you have decided on where you want to crop the picture you can then scale it by taking the measurements of the picture you have and then deciding what shape and size of frame you will want on the page. You can then calculate the percentage increase or reduction required to fit the picture into the frame on the page. In other words, if the cropped area of your picture is 22 cm wide by 15 cm deep and you want it to fit in a frame that is 15 cm wide, then the image will be 68 per cent of the original. This means that the 15 cm depth will reduce to 10.2 cm in the final image. Your frame should therefore be 15 cm wide by 10.2 cm deep (see Figure 10.6).

Ethics and pictures

Now that picture desks have become fully electronic there is little that you can't do to edit a picture. Take off a person's hat? Easy. Bring two people closer together? The stroke of a cursor key. This raises considerable ethical questions.

Occasionally a picture will require re-touching by artists to remove blemishes or to cover up identification marks on vehicles. It can sometimes be tempting to use such re-touching to change a picture. This should be avoided.

It's very important to take care with library pictures. If you are using a picture of a person or landmark, check that the picture is still up to date. Using a picture of someone as they looked ten or even twenty years before will not be too helpful. If that is the only picture, then you might decide to still use it but you should always make it clear that the picture is out of date. Pictures have often been used in newspapers when the police are searching for a missing person that looks very little like the person being sought. Extra information could make all the difference: 'The missing person pictured happily at home a few years ago when her hair was still brown and not blonde', makes it clear that the picture is out of date and that the missing woman's hair colour has changed.

The same is true of landmarks. If it is essential to use a picture of a landmark that is out of date (a nearby building that has been demolished, for instance) and a new picture can't be taken or the existing picture cropped to fit the new circumstances, then the only sensible approach is to make it clear the picture is a library picture and so is out of date.

Figure 10.6 The original picture needs to be scaled so that the final image is smaller at only 8 cm high. This means reducing to 66 per cent. We can either calculate the width (66 per cent of 9 cm is 6 cm) or we can draw a diagonal through the picture, draw a vertical line of 8 cm (the height of our final image) and then measure the horizontal line, to find the width

Special effects

Occasionally a picture needs to be changed to get the full effect required. This change could involve flipping the picture so that what was the right-hand edge, becomes the left. This allows a picture to face into the page that would otherwise be facing out. It is a technique that needs to be handled with care. Hair partings, moles and scars now appear on the wrong side and those are the subtle signs that give away a flipped picture. You can also change a picture to lay a texture over it, bleach the picture or change the tonal values in some other way so that you can disguise some part of the picture, perhaps. You can also paste two or more pictures together, to give the appearance of a much wider picture area. It is possible to darken a picture leaving only the area we want the reader to concentrate on at the normal brightness and contrast (see Figure 10.3). All of these effects could be used to illustrate a story.

There is a discussion of the ethics of interfering with pictures in Chapter 9, but with modern software such as Photoshop you can do almost anything to a picture. To illustrate a feature about soccer hooligans for instance, you might

Figure 10.7 Filters can dramatically change the look of a photograph. Left: normal; Right top: coloured pencil; Left bottom: dry brush; right bottom: mezzotint

want a large picture of an after-match riot. You may have one in the library, but that would be of a specific news event and it might put you at risk of a libel suit if the participants' identities were obvious. By texturing the picture or bleaching it (see Figure 10.7) to remove the tones leaving only black and white, the impression of a riot might be left (or even improved, stark black and white might be better than photographic realism) without identifying people and leaving the paper at risk of a libel suit.

A feature on divorce, for example, might be illustrated with a wedding picture torn down the middle. Getting a wedding picture from the library would do, but the identities of the couple would need to be disguised in some way.

This kind of interference with pictures is acceptable, but it is also possible to make major changes to pictures using Photoshop and a kind of manipulation that could mean you risk having a picture that is untruthful and therefore unethical.

Graphics

Graphics have become even more important these days. The use of computer systems has allowed quick and easy access to graphic packages that can easily be placed on a page to illustrate a story. Whether it's a pile of cash to make a breaker on a budget day story, or a drawing of a plane taking off to illustrate a holiday story, there's plenty of material about. What is more difficult is specially drawn artwork. This will normally be produced by the art department, but you will need to brief them about what you want and when you need it. The quality of work they can offer may well depend on the amount of time they have, so it is worth deciding on a graphic as soon as possible. Any story involving a clear grasp of special locations is worth considering for graphics. Anything with figures or a large amount of detail might also benefit from a graphical interpretation (see Figure 10.8 for an example).

Finally, any story without any other good pictures should be considered for a graphic. Figure 10.9 shows a graphic I have produced to illustrate my point. It takes two fairly limited pictures, one of the 'victim' and one of the 'scene' and ties them into a graphic to show where the 'body' was found only a short distance from where the 'victim' went missing.

Figure 10.8 (overleaf top) A graphic using photographs to offer the reader more information about an archaeological dig

Figure 10.9 (overleaf bottom) A picture graphic

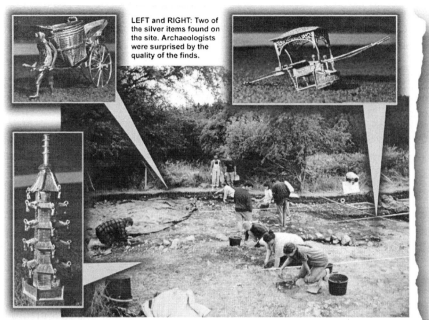

LEFT and RIGHT: Two of the silver items found on the site. Archaeologists were surprised by the quality of the finds.

ABOVE LEFT: A silver tower found on the site. ABOVE RIGHT: The main dig site at a secret location. Archaeologists believe it might be the site of a Roman palace.

11.35pm: a man is seen running up Leonard St shortly after witnesses heard screams. He was wearing a red fleece and dark trousers.

Emma Ferguson's body was found the next morning. A back gate had been broken open and her body had been dragged into the back garden.

11
Using colour

Colour plays a major part in our lives because we have well developed colour vision, yet colour has come only relatively recently to newspapers and even magazines have only been published in full colour for about thirty years. Much of this move towards colour was driven by advertisers. According to Favre and November (1979: 80) surveys amongst consumers showed a marked improvement in attention getting when colour was used:

	Four-colour ads %	Black and white ads %
The ad was seen	57	43
The brand was identified	43	28
The text was read	22	16

With figures like these, it is no surprise that advertisers were clamouring for publications to switch to full colour as soon as possible and so even newspapers that resisted moving to colour because they feared it would damage their brand image, making them appear more populist and frivolous, were eventually obliged to introduce it.

Our eyes are receptive to light through cells in the retinas called rods and cones. Rods perceive the relative brightness of a light wave and are not influenced at all by its colour while cones detect the hue of the light wave telling the brain how much red, green and blue light energy there is. Each cone detects all the colours, but some are much more receptive to one part of the colour spectrum than another and this allows us to detect the difference between various colours. Our cones are particularly receptive to red, green or blue, according the theories of Helmholtz (cited in De Grandis 1986: 14), and we detect other colours by measuring how much red, green or blue is contained in them. The wavelength of 570 mµ for instance stimulates the red, green and blue cones in a ratio of 2:7:7 to give the impression of pure yellow (ibid.)

Colour comes to exist when light bounces off an object. That object will contain a pigment that absorbs some of the light in a particular colour range. What is left is then reflected back to us, or, in the case of a transparent material, passes straight through. White paper absorbs little of the light and reflects nearly all of it back. Black objects absorb the majority of light. Colour doesn't exist in a dark room, because if there is no light, there is no colour. A wall might be painted with a pigment that reflects only green, but if there is no light to reflect, then it is black.

Because we see red, green and blue light, television sets also use this RGB principle. TV sets have three guns that emit light, one red, one blue and one green. These colours then combine to give the impression of a variety of colours. White light is made up of appropriate proportions of those three colours. If we split white light into its components using a prism then we get a spectrum of colours starting in the infra-red area going red, orange, yellow, green, blue, indigo, violet and ultra violet.

HUE, SATURATION AND VALUE

As well as the actual colour being displayed, the hue, we need to be aware that there are other ways of altering how we perceive colour. We may like a nice red, but we might prefer it lighter or brighter, or duller or darker. Hue is the type of colour being described. In good light, you can distinguish up to 500 different hues.

The saturation (or chroma or intensity) is the amount of that hue. In printing 100 per cent would be complete colour, 0 per cent would be grey; no colour at all. A very dense colour has a high saturation value, a low saturation value would give a grey muddy colour. A stormy day prevents the transmission of light from an object and mixes it with light reflected from moisture in the atmosphere and so things in the distance tend to look grey and washed out.

Value (or lightness or brightness or tone) is the relative brightness of a colour. As a colour's value approaches 100 per cent it becomes whiter, at 100 per cent it is white. At 0 per cent it is black.

The value will determine how vibrant a colour is. Look out on a bright sunny day, and often the colours look washed out because the white light reflects and makes colours look lighter. Take a walk after a rainstorm during the day and the colours will look bright and vibrant as the light gives a value of 50 per cent. At night the low light levels do not give your eyes enough information. The value is low and things will tend to look black.

PSYCHOLOGY OF COLOUR

Colour is very important to us and its effect on our lives is significant. Colours are associated with emotions. Blue is calming but cold. Yellows and reds are associated with warmth and speed. Greens are more neutral and are considered nurturing. Rooms in which you spend time should be green or beige or brown. Value is important too. Rooms with bright light tend to have vibrant colours or are tending towards white. Rooms with soft lighting will reduce the colour value to make the hues less threatening.

RANK

Colour plays a part in everyday social interaction with rank and place often being designated by colour. School uniforms are coloured as are the outfits of sports teams. Rank can be defined by colour as in the bishop's purple and the scarlet of a Roman Catholic cardinal. Political parties define themselves by colour and many companies these days oblige their staff to wear uniforms designed in the company's brand colours.

SYMBOLISM

Colours are also symbolic. We all recognise the red and yellow of fire, the blue of water and the green of nature. Map makers use these colours to mark out tracts of water or forest. We would be more likely to use green on a gardening column than red.

Red is easy to spot and so was used on telephone kiosks and post boxes until recently. Consequently red came to symbolise the post office. Yellow is often used to represent Easter and red and green are traditionally symbolic of Christmas.

COLOUR INTERACTIONS

Objects of the same colour look different depending on their setting. The light reflected back into a room will be affected by the colour they are reflected from. A blue surround will add a blue hue to a white object while a red background would give it a red hue. Different colours together give each other different properties.

This effect can be extended. If you work for any length of time on a computer with a monochrome green screen, your eyes' red receptors are underused. Seeing something red soon after will make it appear more intense than usual. If you have an unusual and vibrant colour scheme on your computer desktop, you've probably noticed this effect.

Some colours, called complementary colours, work well with others making them stand out better. It is no surprise that baked beans are packed in a tin with a blue-green label. The blue-green is on the opposite side of the colour wheel (a theoretical circle of colours that artists use to guide them in the use of colour) to orange. The blue-green makes the orange of the beans look more vibrant and appetising. Green would also have helped emphasise the orange (although not as well as the blue-green), but as green is the colour of mould, it is usually avoided in food packaging.

COLOUR SEPARATION

Although TV, computers and our eyes work on the red/green/blue principle, this additive method (where different colours of light are added together) does not work for printing. Paints are pigments so that the red paint allows only red light to be reflected. If we mixed blue paint (that only allowed blue light to reflect) with green paint (that allowed only green paint to reflect) and red paint (that only allowed red light to be reflected, then no light would be reflected and the colour would appear to be black.

The printing process also uses pigments – inks that essentially lay down a series of colour filters, which don't add, but subtract colours. The printing of the colour red merely subtracts all other colours from reflecting from that area of paper. Adding green and red light together on a TV screen gives yellow. If you were to mix green and red paint (or ink) you would filter all light except that which could filter through the two coloured inks and you would get a muddy brown. Additive colour principles use the presence of light in all three primary colours to produce white and their absence to produce black.

When we are using pigments, we are not adding light together, we are subtracting light by preventing it from reflecting from the pigment surface. In traditional colour theory, as used by artists, there are three pigment colours that cannot be mixed from other colours and so are considered primaries: red, blue and yellow (Zelanski and Fisher 1989: 15). By mixing the primaries, you get secondary colours. Mixing red and blue gives purple, blue and yellow gives green and yellow and red gives orange. However, we are not working with paint when we print, we are working with transparent pigments of ink (the same applies to the transparent pigments of colour photography). This allows us to use the secondary colours given by the additive principles although we must use ink in a subtractive way, filtering out colours rather than adding them as we can do with light on a TV set.

The subtractive principle uses filters to represent the secondary colours of cyan, magenta and yellow that we would get if we were mixing coloured light. Mixing red and blue gives magenta, mixing red and green gives yellow and mixing green and blue gives cyan. When all these secondary colours are present, they print black, when all are absent they print white (provided you are using white paper).

Add yellow and cyan inks together and you will get the primary colour of green because the inks will have reflected only yellow light (a mix of red and green) and cyan light (a mix of blue and green). Since the yellow pigment will have absorbed the blue light reflected by the cyan pigment and the cyan pigment will have absorbed the red light reflected by the yellow pigment, only green light is left to be reflected. Remember, the inks are transparent so one does not block the reflecting power of the other, only filters it, so the green light can reflect through both pigments. If the pigment were paint, it would not reflect through both. We make paint to cover over all the colours beneath the top layer.

Although the secondary ink colours used for printing are magenta, cyan and yellow, black is normally used as well. This is because of deficiencies in inks. Although the theory says combining the secondary colours should give black, in fact the best possible is a muddy brown. The addition of black ink allows the printer to produce pure black and to alter the value of the colours from full black to white. The black can then be used to print the black type that still tends to be used for text ensuring that the printer doesn't have to struggle to get the four colour plates in register to print the delicate type. Imagine trying to represent black type by laying four colours, one on top of the other for six point type. It is much easier to use black, which will also give much better results. Black is represented by the letter K so this four-colour process system is often known as the CMYK system.

USE OF COLOUR IN PRINT

Colour is now widely used in print. Years ago it was an expensive and therefore little used luxury. Magazines switched to serious use of colour in the 1970s and they were followed by newspapers towards the end of the 1980s. There are now very few provincial or national papers not making extensive use of full or process colour.

There are two main areas for colour use: pictures and tonal variety. Both are important but for different things. If we were producing a fashion spread for instance, it would be vital that the pictures were in full colour so that the reader could get the full effect of the fashion. Pictures of carnivals or theatrical productions also tend to look good in colour.

On the other hand, a TV listings page might not need colour for the pictures or graphics but could be made much easier to read by using colour to separate out items from each other. Colour patches could be put behind each channel listing so that a light yellow might emphasise the ITV channel while a light pink could be used to support BBC1, for instance.

This means that if we have a colour page, we should be considering not only whether we are using colour or monochrome pictures, but how we are going to use colour to support both the pictures and the text.

Colour is particularly useful in tone patches, rules, boxes and highlights. It tends to be less useful in display faces and type, or at least for any length of type. A drop cap or a small crosshead can look good in colour but at the end of the day, we have to remember that we are trying to help not hinder the reader and a long run of coloured text, particularly if the value (or lightness) is very high, is not going to be easy to read.

Black on white is still the easiest way to present type and to read it and you change that at your peril. Using coloured paper, coloured type or a heavy type patch often reduces legibility. In tests carried out by Karl Borggräfe (cited in Favre and November 1979: 50) to see which colours worked best together, the following taxonomy of colour mixes was discovered, starting with the most legible and working through to the least legible.

Black on yellow	Black on red
Yellow on black	Blue on orange
Green on white	Yellow on green
Red on white	Blue on red
Black on white	Yellow on red
White on blue	White on red
Blue on yellow	Red on black
Blue on white	White on orange
White on black	Black on green
Green on yellow	Orange on white
Black on orange	Orange on blue
Red on yellow	Yellow on orange
Orange on black	Red on orange
Yellow on blue	Red on green
White on green	Green on orange

As you can see, black and white comes pretty near the top although, the list suggests that a yellow panel behind the black type would improve legibility (which is why important signs warning of danger are usually printed black on yellow). This choice of colour is clearly one that would work well, but remember that the yellow panel we could provide in a newspaper would have a heavy dot screen and this might not improve legibility. Magazines normally have better quality paper and so a finer raster dot and this effect would be less noticeable than in a newspaper. In both types of publication, however, you need to be careful about reversing type out of a colour background, because if the type is too small it will be swamped by the raster dots of the background.

Mixes of red and green or orange and green were seen as the worst in the list above with blue and red close behind. This might be, in part at least, because red, blue and green have slightly different focal lengths. This means the eye cannot focus on all the colours at the same time. This leaves the edges of the letters a little fuzzy and this can be both disconcerting and hard to read.

COLOUR AS DEFINITION

Colour can help you define an area whether it is text or picture. The Poynter Institute's Eye-trac research shows that colour draws a reader into a page (Garcia and Stark 1991). Colour can be used in pictures, in text or as a background colour. Placing type on a patch of light yellow pulls that text away from the surrounding white paper and certainly sets it apart from another block of text set on a light red patch.

It is tempting when you first start using colours to use big bright splashes of colour, but this can be a bad idea. Apart from making it difficult to print – large areas of heavy colour take longer to dry and are more likely to cause problems on the press – these big areas of colour compete with each other for the reader's attention. They can make a page look over-busy. Colour often looks better in light shades that draw the eye, but don't dominate it. This is particularly true in newspapers where there is little space to be wasted. The page needs to be filled with type or pictures and so colours have to be directly involved with the picture or the type. Heavy colour patches beneath type makes black type difficult to read and I've already warned about reversing type out of colour patches. Laying colour against pictures also needs to be done with care. Putting a border around a picture can be helpful if the colour used matches a key colour of the subject, because it will help emphasise the subject, but using a colour that pulls away from the subject is not helpful, unless it is a complementary colour that again will emphasise the colour of the subject.

Drop caps can be printed in a strong colour as can side-heads or crossheads. Captions, bylines or standfirsts can be made to stand away from the rest of the page by printing them in colour. It's best to use a hue with a relatively low saturation and a low value so that the colour has a strong density that makes it stand away from the text without being over-vibrant.

It is also possible to use gradient patches. Gradients are where the patch starts at one value and across the width or depth of the patch changes to another value, so the patch might start light and end up dark. A gradient patch can also start out as light in the centre and end up dark at the edges or vice versa. As well as changing the lightness, you can also change the hue or the saturation (or all three) through a gradient to give a number of effects that will add emphasis to certain parts of the page.

COLOUR AS BRAND IMAGE

An important use of colour is as a brand image. Coca-Cola's brilliant red is perhaps one of the more famous examples of a brand colour, but there are plenty of other organisations and corporations, not to mention nations, that use colour as a brand or identity.

Your own publication might well have corporate colours that need to be included in the publication. This would be particularly true if you are producing a publication for a company to be distributed amongst customers or employees. We regularly identify things by colour and these colours should be included in a publication.

It also means that we might need to be careful about using certain colours on a particular story. If we were designing a page on personal finance for instance, there might well be an advert for an insurance company near this that would be published in that company's corporate colours. We should therefore try to avoid using that combination of colours on the page to ensure that the editorial was not linked with the advert.

However, to run a travel item about America using red, white and blue, or an Italian food feature using red, green and white would be a perfectly sensible thing to do as the symbolism involved would be immediately recognised by most people and it would emphasise the national identity.

12
Publishing ethics

Ethics in journalism start from the moment a reporter asks his or her first question. From then on, everything a journalist does should be guided by his or her professional morality. This doesn't necessarily mean that there is only one standard that applies to all. Professional morality may vary depending on who one is working for. The morality on the *Sun* may be different to the morality applied on the *Guardian*. Whether one is better than the other is for the individual to judge. That said, there are some basic standards laid down in the Press Complaints Commission's (PCC's) code of practice and the National Union of Journalist's code of conduct.

There is not enough space here for an in depth discussion about professional morality and ethics. There are several books that discuss journalistic ethics (Frost 2000, Keeble 2001, Kieran 1998) if you want to know more. For the purposes of this chapter it is assumed that you will want to consider the journalistic virtues of fairness, responsibility and truth in all your professional work.

ETHICS OF DISPLAY AND DESIGN

Designers and editors do not particularly need to consider the morality of gathering news. They are presented with stories already sourced and written. Sub-editors of course will want to reassure themselves that the codes of practice have been adhered to and if there are any apparent breaches, a good sub will approach the news editor or the reporter concerned to discuss the matter. If this does not resolve things to the sub's satisfaction he or she should raise the matter with the chief sub or if necessary, the editor.

Provided the copy is ethically based however, very few of the code of practice clauses apply to the ethics of design and publication.

The PCC's code covers:

1. Accuracy	9. Hospitals
2. Opportunity to reply	10. Reporting of crime
3. Privacy	11. Misrepresentation
4. Harassment	12. Victims of sexual assault
5. Intrusion into grief or shock	13. Discrimination
6. Children	14. Financial journalism
7. Children in sex cases	15. Confidential sources
8. Listening devices	16. Payment for articles

Provided the copy offered for publication has adhered to these code elements in itself, you can see that there is little directly in the code for the designer to worry about. But this does not mean that there are no ethical dilemmas for the designer – far from it.

The main areas of concern are: has any additional text been dealt with fairly? Are captions accurate? Do headlines avoid sensationalising the copy? Have pictures been unfairly manipulated? Has undue pressure been brought to bear on whether to use the copy or spike it? Perhaps there has been pressure to cut the story or use it on a particular page. Perhaps an advertiser would like it to lie alongside a particular advert.

Are the pictures a true and accurate reflection of what took place? Have they been manipulated unfairly? Are they appropriate to use in this context? Does your publisher own the appropriate rights to whatever it is you are thinking of publishing? Are the copy and/or pictures being used suitable for the audience to whom they are being offered.

COPYRIGHT

Copyright, as with so many things, is both an ethical and legal matter. Essentially there are two main rights involved with copyright:

1. Moral rights – that is the right to determine whether copy or pictures are used and whether they can be altered.

2. Intellectual property rights – the right to make money from the copy or pictures by selling them, or the right to publish them, to people.

These two rights are separate and different. I can sell my intellectual property rights to any one I want; I can even give them away. I cannot sell my moral rights. In the UK, the Copyright, Designs and Patents Act 1988 protects the moral rights of authors, photographers and other creative workers. If you produce a piece of creative work you have the right to be identified as the author; the right not to have work subjected to derogatory treatment; and the right for every person not to have work falsely attributed to them (Carey 1996: 106). Much of this does not apply to those who write for magazines or newspapers, however. A reporter does not have a cause for action just because he or she did not get a byline. The writers of books, music or plays do have such rights.

Since news reporters do not have any moral rights over their work, they often forget that other creative workers might. So if you want to use a photograph, or quote a poem or the lyrics to your favourite song, you need to be certain you are not breaching someone's copyright. Even TV programme titles are subject to copyright and it is not unknown for the BBC's lawyers to send a sharp letter to a newspaper using a programme title in a headline on a story that is not about that programme.

However, the property rights involved in an intellectual work can be sold, so it is possible to buy the right to use a picture, song lyrics or a story. A freelance reporter may not have the moral right to insist on a byline or prevent derogatory treatment, but they do own the copyright and can therefore sell it to anyone they wish. They can sell it for ever or they can sell a licence to use it. Normally a freelance would want to keep the copyright so that the right to use the story can be resold to another outlet.

For instance, a freelance reporter might have covered an interesting court case and being the only freelance there he or she might then sell the story to a number of newspapers and magazines. None of these would own the copyright, which would stay with the reporter (although they would have copyright in the typographical arrangement of that page), but they would be allowed to use the story in that edition of the paper. The reporter might then seek additional payment if the paper wanted to put the story on its website or syndicate it to other newspapers around the world.

Although much of this work is standardised, you need to be certain what it is you are buying should you negotiate with a freelance or agency for their copy or pictures. Do they own the rights and are you buying just what you need? There's no point in buying rights to publish on the website if you don't have a website.

Things are not always in the seller's favour. Many newspapers and other news outlets now attempt to take all rights from freelances by sending a cheque for submitted work that has a stamp on the back saying that cashing the cheque accepts that the news outlet now owns all copyright rights on the piece of work. The National Union of Journalists has been very busy over the past ten years trying to negotiate acceptable settlements to prevent what it describes as a 'rights grab'. Although it has many deals with publishers, there are still quite a few multi-national corporations who pay fees appropriate to single first use of copyright material and then attempt to take all future rights over the material as well.

It is always important to check who owns the copyright. For instance, when something newsworthy happens, such as the murder of a young child, reporters often try to get pictures from relatives. The picture offered might be one of those standard school pictures. They are usually the best quality and show the child looking clean and well-scrubbed. The copyright on these is usually owned by the photographic studio and if you use it without checking, you may well be breaching the studio's copyright – something for which they can sue your paper.

Often photographs such as school photos, wedding photos, photos taken on cruise ships, night clubs or holidays are copyright of the photographer. They are the only ones entitled to make copies of the work, which is how they make their money – selling prints to customers. You are not entitled to make copies without permission. Check with them first and negotiate a copyright payment. Remember that the market rate applies and a rare photograph might be very expensive. One-off photographs of celebrities doing things they shouldn't be doing or other one-off news events where there is only one picture can net the copyright holder hundreds of thousands of pounds and continue to be a good earner for years to come. The clip of film of John F. Kennedy being assassinated in Dallas was recently the subject of a court case to establish ownership by the family of the man who took it – it was said to be worth millions of dollars. Another recent case involved the picture of Che Guevara which had become an emblem of revolution through the sixties. The photographer had been happy for it to be used to support revolution, but had not been happy when it had been picked up for commercial gain by a drinks company and he sued. Both cases netted the copyright holders millions of dollars. It is likely that the amateur videos of the September 11 attacks on New York's twin towers could also earn their copyright holders millions.

The main defence we have against suits for infringement of copyright is fair dealing. Fair dealing is where the copyright material was used for the purposes of reporting current events or criticism or review, provided it is accompanied by a suitable acknowledgement. Therefore there is no problem about reporting a speech by the prime minister made in public since we would be clearly acknowledging who said what. If the speech was made in private and the media was refused permission to report it, we might have more of a problem. A speaker does have copyright over his or her speech. However, provided it was in the public interest, we could report the substance of the speech and perhaps even use sections of it. According to Carey the 'courts have shown a willingness, in exceptional cases, to allow a defendant to avail himself. . .' of the defence of public interest when reproducing a speech (Carey 1996: 106).

Fair dealing means acknowledging the source. If, for instance, you were reviewing a play, it would be acceptable to publish a small section, provided you made it clear that that is what it was and who wrote it. You might also use stills from a movie in order to support a review. Again these need to acknowledge the film and its director. In practice of course, the movie-makers would normally provide you with a press pack that would include pictures for you to use free of copyright payments.

PLAGIARISM

This is similar to stealing copyright in that it involves passing off the work of others as your own. In these cases it is often less clear that the work belongs to someone else. The work may have been rewritten or it may involve stealing someone else's ideas. There is no copyright on ideas or on news events. If there is a big fire in your town and an opposition paper published news about it first, they cannot then sue you for copyright if your paper also publishes a story about it – unless you use their story or pictures. However, it is not unknown for journalists to rewrite someone else's story or to lift pieces of copy. Often this will be done because one paper or magazine was able to interview someone that the other publication did not get to. Lifting the quotes and using them in your own publication is plagiarism. Plagiarism is a difficult area. Few people would consider misquoting the Chancellor of the Exchequer in a story about the budget just because the misquotes were taken from live TV or a radio broadcast. Taking photographs of a live TV broadcast is also often considered fair game and many publications have used pictures of major live events taken from TV transmissions. It is fair dealing that allows us to use such pictures, or use the TV as the source. Taking photographs from the television of a live transmission of a news event, provided the pictures are acknowledged is now well within existing case law (Carey 1996: 105). Publishing a list of classified information from another publication would not be covered by fair dealing. If your rival (or the local Yellow Pages) published a list of local restaurants and your publication simply copied this list and presented it as their own, this would be both plagiarism and breach of copyright. (For further advice see Mason and Smith 1998: 102.)

EDITING PICTURES

Editing pictures carries the same duties and responsibilities as editing text. Inevitably you are going to have to make editorial decisions. There is no such thing as an objective picture. A photographer has had to decide which pictures to take, where to point the camera, what to frame and when to open the shutter. He or she then has to decide which pictures to offer to the picture desk. Once the editor has them, he or she has to decide which pictures to use, how many, how they will be cropped and what size they will be (see Figure 12.1).

That said, it is very easy these days to alter a picture to show whatever you want. Modern photographic software makes it easy to make major changes to a picture. One famous example involves the *Sun*. It carried a story on the front page about a monk who had fallen in love with a woman and had been asked to resign. They obtained a picture of the monk and the woman walking down the street. But they were not close and the man was in ordinary clothes. In an attempt to make the story clearer, the *Sun* manipulated the picture to show the man wearing a monk's habit, holding the woman's hand. The *Sun* later admitted: 'We have superimposed the monk's habit to make it clear to the readers that the story is about a monk' (Frost 2000: 137) (see Figure 12.2 for a picture that has been changed).

Figure 12.1 The original picture (top left) can present several different stories – so which one is true?

Figure 12.2 A picture can be altered to a very large extent. But is it ethical to change a picture as much as this? Removing the defenders alters the reality

But even if a picture is not manipulated, it can still distort the truth. A simple example involves the party conferences. Each year the political parties gather at the seaside to discuss policy and to hear a rousing speech from their leader. Photographers take thousands of pictures of the leader and other key party figures. Even if they are just sitting on the platform, their expression can be very telling and can be used to illustrate a point. During the late 1990s, several photographers managed to get a picture of former Tory leaders Margaret Thatcher and Edward Heath sitting close to each other listening to William Hague, then leader of the Conservative Party, make his speech. Both were caught coincidentally looking at their watches with expressions of apparent boredom. It was a picture that made several of the newspapers, and was being used as a comment on the new leader's speech.

Politicians soon learn to take extreme care about their hand gestures and facial expressions when in public. Any major politician making a speech soon learns that there is little that can be done to prevent the press choosing an image to suit their message. When a major politician makes a speech, each photographer will take scores of pictures. This ensures that the news desk will get the kind of expression they want. This will either be a picture to match the tone of the speech, or a picture to match the tone of the report. Choosing the right picture can change the truth of the story and is an important editorial and ethical decision.

Pictures themselves can be unethical and so should not be used. The *Hartlepool Mail* was criticised by the PCC in 1997 for using a picture of a child taken at a funeral as it breached the PCC's code on children (PCC 1997 vol. 40). Any picture taken with a long lens should be considered carefully before use – the PCC may well require the editor to explain why using the picture was in the public interest, while any picture taken of the subject in a private place should be considered very, very carefully before use. The PCC will almost always take the view that such pictures should not be used. In one recent case a photograph was taken inside a cafe for an advertising feature. A customer complained his privacy had been invaded and the complaint was upheld.

EDITING TEXT

Editing text can also alter the truth. A certain amount of editing becomes inevitable. Stories are too long for the space available, priorities change and a good story may have been overtaken by an even better story. This means the story as written by the reporter may need to be cut. It may also need to be merged with a story from a different reporter or it might need to be split into three or four stories to be presented in the way the editor has decided. Even if the copy is largely untouched, it needs to be checked and facts confirmed if there are doubts. All of this means that the text used will be different to the text offered. Since the offered text will already be full of subjective decisions made by the reporter, it is possible that the sub-editor is taking the copy even further from the truth by amending it again. It is by no means unusual for a reporter to build up a story as much as he or she dares – stretching the truth close to breaking point – only for a sub-editor to take the story and assuming that the story is straightforward, stretch it even further; taking the elements the reporter has hinted at and making them appear to be unarguable fact.

Not only can a sub put mistakes and unethical elements into a story, but he or she is also be responsible for removing them. While it will not always possible to spot errors of fact or be able to tell if the reporter was unethical in gathering a story, text that is clearly comment or is discriminatory should be removed. For instance, the PCC upheld a complaint in 1997 against *Time Out* which had run an article about 'sitting next to the "nutter on the bus"'. The PCC said this was not in the spirit of its guidance on mental illness (PCC 1997 vol. 40).

Headlines

Headlines are one of the main trouble spots for fair reporting. The headline is there to sell the story, but often it goes much further than the story would allow. When writing a headline a sub-editor needs to be very careful that it does not become sensationalist or inaccurate. A number of complaints made to the PCC concern headlines rather than stories.

Headlines, captions, standfirsts and any rewritten material can also breach the PCC's code of conduct in terms of accuracy, discrimination and intrusion. It is new copy and although the facts have been gathered by another person it is very easy for an over-eager sub to introduce errors in the new text. Since it is often the headline or even a caption that the reader sees first, errors here can have more impact than errors in the story.

TASTE AND DECENCY

Taste and decency is a difficult area and not one that is covered by the PCC. The PCC has taken the view that matters of taste and decency are outside its area of responsibility and it is probably right to do so. When it comes to factual publications, questions of taste and decency involve nudity, bad language, depictions of sexual activity, war, terror and other forms of violence. It has to be accepted that controlling these is easier for newspapers and magazines than it is for television, which has the whole range of factual and fictional programmes to contend with.

The main problem area for publications is pictures: pictures of naked people, pictures of sexual activity, pictures of violence and pictures of a bizarre and possibly distasteful nature. Although pictures of this sort have always been seen as a problem of morality, it is not morality that we normally measure when trying to decide whether to use such pictures or articles. In the end it comes down to the audience and this makes life much easier. Instead of a long debate about whether it is right to censor such material or wrong to try to titillate the audience, provided the publication is attempting to present the truth without glorifying it or commercialising it, then the right line will usually be taken. Showing pictures of the aftermath of a terrorist bomb with pictures of the dead and mutilated may make difficult reading, but they do spell out the truth of what happens in such horrific circumstances. On the other hand, inventing a story about people's supposed 'sexploits' on holiday destination aircraft illustrated by pictures of topless 'air hostesses' is the sort of *Sport* commercialisation of sex that appeals, thankfully, to only a small market.

Ignoring the fringe publications such as the *Sport* or *Bizarre*, which make a point of using such material in a titillating way, most publications know that it is the sensibilities of their audience that determines how far they can go in the presentation of nudity, violence, bad language and sex.

Cases of complaint in the past have included stories about inquests that contain too many details; pictures of decapitated heads or executions in various African civil wars; a burnt out Iraqi tank with the dead commander still at his post in the turret; naked children fleeing a napalm attack in Vietnam. All of these were used in various publications and were either supported or criticised. But all of them said something about the truth of the story and, although they may have pushed the limits of their readers' sense of good taste, most understood the reason for using them.

Bad language, when used in quotations and sourced, may also be acceptable, depending on the readership. What one could use in *Loaded* or *Cosmopolitan*, is not what may be acceptable in the local weekly – it's all down to the readership.

CONFLICTS OF INTEREST

Conflicts of interest can occur for a number of reasons. *Copy approval* has long been a feature of A-list celebrity interviews, but the idea is creeping further down the chain. A letter to *Press Gazette* in July 2002 from a sub-editor of a trade magazine asked other sub-editors if they had been instructed by their editors to give copy approval. The letter explained that this particular trade magazine gave copy approval on articles about key figures in that industry.

While it is not unusual, and is probably good practice to check quotes with an interviewee, it is not acceptable to give copy approval. This automatically implies that the person has the right to change the copy and few can resist doing so. This means the copy ceases to be the publication's view of the truth and becomes the source's view of the truth. While we journalists have to accept that the view we give is one-dimensional (ours) we are attempting to be fair and present all sides of the truth and give a rounded report. This is not something the source is concerned about. Their only viewpoint, ethically, practically and commercially is to present themselves in the best possible light. The problem with copy approval is that it is a vicious circle. If access to certain key players – whether A-list celebrities or captains of industry – is limited by copy approval, then stories that do not have approval will be published only rarely. Access to these people for interview will be limited to those prepared to toe the line. As more and more publications give in to copy approval, so more and more sources will ask for copy approval and more and more publications will be obliged to give copy approval. In the end, copy about anything that people actually want to read about will be nothing more than sanitised public relations.

Pressure from advertisers

Pressure from advertisers can be for something as relatively innocuous as asking for a positive story on the company to sit alongside an advertisement to asking for changes in the copy or copy approval. This can be the case particularly in *advertising features*, where the advertiser is paying for space alongside editorial material. The Newspaper Society advises publications to put 'advertising feature' in reasonably sized type over any page that has editorial tied to advertising, but this does not stop the advertiser from thinking they have bought the editorial as well as the advertising space. Once, when designing and subbing an advertising feature, the advertiser rang and demanded to be read the copy. I politely refused but they were insistent and said they would pull the ad if they were not read the copy even though they claimed they did not intend to change the copy. I pointed out that if they did not intend to change it then why did they need it read to them? In the end I refused and they said they would pull the ad. I immediately told the editor (a vital thing to do in the circumstances, the final decision is always the editor's). To his credit he supported my decision even though the advert was pulled. I'm sure he had to take some flack for it later and it was a brave decision.

There is also a more general concern with advertising. Most publications depend heavily on advertising for their commercial success. This can make them nervous of carrying stories about advertisers or potential advertisers. This leads to an implicit pressure not to carry stories that attack advertisers.

Pressure from proprietors

There is often pressure from proprietors or editors to protect advertisers from adverse publicity. They may also want to protect another part of the organisation from bad publicity or to promote another aspect of the organisation. Again the pressure here might be direct or implied. The *Sun* and *The Times*, for instance, are owned by Rupert Murdoch, who also owns *BSkyB*. The number of plugs for *BSkyB* carried in the *Sun* and *The Times* as news led to *Private Eye* carrying a regular column called 'I BspyB', which published plugs for *BSkyB* carried in the copy of the *Sun* or *The Times*.

Many publications are now owned by larger corporations which have other holdings that they would like plugged from time to time. There is also the question of personal contacts. Many proprietors or editors are members of the establishment. This can be a double-edged sword. They know the right people, they mix with them and this is good for business and its good for news gathering, but it also means that they get to know people and may be asked for favours: to publish or sometimes, to not publish.

When working for local papers, it is very difficult not to be involved in the local community, nor is it a particularly good idea for a journalist, particularly an editor, to be detached from the local community. Editors send their children to local schools. They belong to local charitable committees and possibly local political parties or campaigning groups. This will also influence what appears in a particular publication.

Bribes and corruption

While accepting a wad of fivers in a brown paper envelope as a bribe is clearly wrong, accepting cheap deals or discounts is not as obvious in being a bribe. Receiving or accepting freebies (free holidays, cars, meals, books or CDs and so on) may be unavoidable – how else could most local newspapers afford to review new cars or holidays without freebies? But you have to consider how this influences the final copy.

DEFAMATION

Defamation is a large part of media law that I can only touch on here. You should ensure you are fully familiar with the law of defamation by reading an appropriate law book or attending a course (see Carey 2000; Crone 1995; Greenwood and Welsh 2000).

The law of defamation is there to protect a person's reputation. It is designed to provide reparation to that person should anyone publish material that might damage their reputation. The aim of the law of defamation is not to prevent publication of material that might be damaging, but to try to repair the damage caused. Since the truth can damage a person's reputation, publishing the truth is not enough as a defence. You must also prove that that it was reasonable to publish that truth. This defence is called *justification*.

Another defence against defamation is called *privilege*. This is where the defamatory remarks are made in a public forum such as parliament, court or a council meeting and the publication concerned reports those remarks in a fair and contemporaneous (timely) manner. This is designed to ensure open reporting of public debate. Parliament could probably not function if its members were at risk of a suit for defamation every time they opened their mouths. Parliament has its own strict rules about what members can say about each other.

In permanent form defamation is known as libel; in non-permanent form it is known as slander. Journalists are usually sued for libel.

Another defence against a suit for defamation is *fair comment*. This is where comments are made in the form of an opinion on facts and are made in fairness and without malice on a matter of public interest. This could be anything from a review of a local amateur dramatic production to an analysis of the Chancellor's latest budget.

If a publication is threatened with the courts over an alleged defamation, an offer of amends can be made. This can be used as a defence in court if the plaintiff refuses to accept. The offer of amends must include a published apology and a payment of compensation. Since the cost of a libel suit is high, this is often the route taken by a publication. Defending a libel suit involves the High Court and costs of solicitors and barristers can easily get into six figures. If you lose, you also have to pay the plaintiff's legal costs and a large payment may be ordered by the court. Losing a high profile libel case can cost several million pounds.

It is important that any slur on the reputation of a person is not included in a headline or caption or any other text written by the designer or sub-editor without approval from the editor. It is not unknown for copy to be legally safe, while the headline leads to a lawsuit. Don't use library clippings to add information to a story, without checking them thoroughly first. Prior publication is not a defence against a libel suit. Consent to publication is a complete defence against a libel suit, so if you can get the person concerned to sign an approval form, that can be useful.

Pictures

Although publishing pictures in news reports doesn't necessarily need the permission of the subject, permission is certainly needed if the pictures haven't been taken in a public place. Always check that a picture was taken in a public place or that permission was given for it to be taken. It can be wise to pixelate out a person's face if it is not important to the picture to ensure that their privacy is not breached. You should pixilate out the number plates of cars or house numbers or names as a matter of course (see Figure 12.3).

You should also be careful of using archive pictures for purposes other than those for which they were taken. Although the permission of a subject is not required, using a picture out of context could lead to complaints or even a lawsuit. One former colleague used an archived wedding photograph to illustrate a divorce by electronically tearing the picture in two. The couple, who still lived happily together, were mortified and a full apology had to be made together with a compensatory payment.

Children

Pictures of children need to be dealt with particularly carefully – there are some strange people out there. Using a picture of a sporting champion or gala queen is fine, but you should be very careful about giving details, particularly addresses. If it is possible for some ill-wisher to find the child's address or phone number the child may well be subjected to offensive phone calls – something most journalists would prefer to avoid. Identifying children involved in stories that concern their welfare also needs to be considered carefully. Often the story is really about the issue involved and identifying the child is unnecessary.

Figure 12.3 Pixilating number plates or house names can spare people embarrassment

Addresses

You should always be careful about publishing addresses, particularly of vulnerable groups. Celebrities are unlikely to be at risk by having their addresses published, but police officers, serving members of the armed forces, judges and others may be at risk if their addresses are published. Others who are at risk include those at pre-published events such as weddings, honeymoons, funerals or other prize-giving ceremonies. Telling people that a particular house is likely to be empty at a certain time is to invite the local burglars around.

13

Design masterclass

The idea of the design masterclass is to look at a range of pages from contemporary publications and examine why they are good examples of their type. I am not suggesting that the examples here are the best pages ever, but that they are good examples of the designer's art produced to deadline to solve specific problems in a pleasing way.

I have tried to pick a range of examples covering newspapers and magazines but I have limited myself to a dozen. These cover news pages in magazines and newspapers, feature pages in both types of publications and some specialist pages such as TV listings, sports pages and beauty pages.

Where possible I have tried to identify detail, but the aim of this section is not to produce a page designer's version of a train spotters-fanzine, but to identify good practice and show how professionals have gone about the job of designing pages that are attractive to readers.

FIGURE 13.1: A TABLOID FRONT PAGE: DAILY MAIL 11 OCTOBER 2002

Front, full colour, tabloid

This *Daily Mail* page is typical of the publication both in its design and its copy-tasting choices. Aimed at a female audience, the story concerns the first birth in the UK from a frozen human egg. The story is the only one run on the page and fills the bottom two thirds of the page. The top third is taken up with the mast head and large *blurb* advertising an inside news feature about how lottery money is spent. This takes a highly polemic standpoint with which the editorial team believes readers will sympathise.

The page is in colour and the blurb is an orangey yellow against a teal blue background. The 'Archer's diaries' and 'Northern Belle' blurbs are white on red. The picture is in full colour, but the rest of the page is black on white.

Figure 13.1   Daily Mail 11 October 2002

The lead heading uses a traditional serif face in about 220pt for the streamer and 42pt for the second deck, which is a seven-line double-column heading. The streamer is very limited for space, despite going across the entire page. Only eleven characters are available for this heading leaving the sub little choice but to go for a label heading; eleven characters are not enough for a subject and a verb, unless you are very lucky. The sub is relying on the second deck to act as both a headline and a standfirst with an extensive fourteen words (about eighty characters). This heading is followed by a discrete byline for the science correspondent. This tends to imply that the copy has a greater authority than would be the case if written by a general news reporter. Underneath the heading is a short double-column take of copy. The entry point is clear, because there is no other copy-sized text on the page. It has a larger sized bold intro with caps start and no indent.

The main picture takes a quarter of the page, filling the bottom right. It is semi-cutout so that the couple stand slightly outside the frame making it appear that they are climbing out of the frame, adding animation and increasing the image size. If the whole picture to be used was the same size as the family, much more room would be required. As it is, the family edge into the 12pt border that surrounds the story and into the caption and heading.

So little copy is used on this page that a *turn-to* line is required, inviting the reader to continue the story on page two. Since there is no other story on page one, this invitation to turn over carries little risk that the reader will turn before finishing other stories on the page. It may even be of some advantage in that they are now more likely to start reading page two and are less likely to drift off to another page and miss the early news pages. This page ideally suits the *Mail's* audience: middle-England women, who hold traditional, establishment views and who are aspiring to a better lifestyle. The chance to produce children on demand at a time that suits them best will both worry their conservative instincts while titillating their aspirational desire to be in control of their lives.

The story is presented in a narrative form that is often seen in the *Daily Mail*. It sits beneath a heading that is presented in a traditional font that is easy to read. The whole page is attractive, well balanced, clear and unequivocal. As with most *Mail* pages it is a fine example of the designer's art and is a model front page.

FIGURE 13.2: A TABLOID PICTURE PAGE: DAILY MIRROR **11 OCTOBER 2002 PAGE 3**

Right-hand page, full colour, tabloid

This *Daily Mirror* page breaks from the traditions of newspaper design and that is one of the reasons why I chose it. The whole page is a giant colour picture of model Sam Fox on the Paris catwalk, playing the part of Sally Bowles as played by Liza Minnelli in the film *Cabaret*. Although there is nothing particularly newsworthy about the story, it is topical and the pictures are nice; they were used by a number of newspapers on the same day. The *Mirror* obviously decided that if you've got it, you should flaunt it and went to town on them. Using the whole picture, they were able to make use of the shaded area down the right to bleed into a black patch. They then overlaid heading, additional pictures and text on the patch. This gives the impression that text and pictures pierce the picture. This impression is enhanced by the white border around the pictures. The headings are in the sans serif font that the *Mirror* normally uses for its pages with the main lead underlined to add emphasis. This emphasis is required because the heading cannot be any larger, without reducing the character count, which is already small at about 8½ characters per line over three lines. The sub goes for a label heading, partly because of this lack of space and partly because it fits the copy which talks about Sam Fox playing the part twenty years after first appearing on the *Sun*'s page three.

The other pictures used are from Sam Fox's early modelling days, one of Liza Minnelli as Sally and one from the same Paris show of Sam Fox with another model. The main picture fills half the width of the page leaving just enough room for the heading, text (only about 200 words) and secondary pictures. There's an excellent feel of balance about the page and the white on black heading and caption are set against the black on white text to hold up the right-hand side of the page against the strong main picture which easily holds our attention on the left. The entry point is clearly signalled by the white patch under the text and the whole page is a lot of fun.

FIGURE 13.3: A TABLOID NEWS PAGE: THE SUN **10 OCTOBER 2002 PAGE 2**

Left-hand page, monochrome, tabloid

This inside news page from the *Sun* takes all the usual virtues one expects from the 'soaraway *Sun*'. It has lively display of interesting but important stories and is probably the *Sun* at its best. There is a very high story count (10) plus the weather and the newsdesk phone numbers.

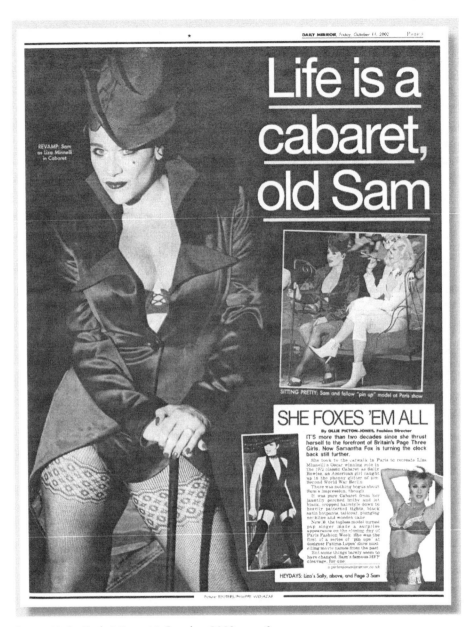

Figure 13.2   Daily Mirror 11 October 2002 page 3

Reverses (white on black headings) are used extensively to compensate for the absence of pictures and graphics. There is only one picture on the page, and although this is a fairly uninteresting portrait of a school building, it is still used across five standard columns. There is a reasonable amount of white space down the sides, which suggests the subs were trying to restrict the depth of the picture on the page while trying to keep the full content of the picture in order to have enough space to lay the two reverse headings over the corners.

Figure 13.3   A tabloid news page: the *Sun* 10 October 2002 page 2

The three-line heading tied in with the two reversed sub-headings makes a strong statement at the centre of the page. This is emphasised by the 2pt border that runs around the story and into the strapline and makes it clear where the entry point is. The text has a bold sans serif intro and it all runs evenly across three equal columns, even thought the space is five columns wide. There is a heavy 'exclusive' tag in the centre and a crosshead halfway down. The blob par about Estelle Morris and the truancy crackdown at the end of the story is a good way of dropping in additional information connected to the story but not actually part of it.

The left-hand column makes use of design repetition to give it strength and the reverse headings with their 'war on terror' tag are placed over bold text. The right-hand side has neat sans serif headings, underlined over light text. The symmetry of the page is picked up with the double column headings over the stories at the base of the page with identical styles being used for the two stories either side of the Lotto results. It's a busy page and one that is full of interest for the reader, with none of the stories being run at too much length. It is not a particularly arty design but it is an excellent use of type, space and colour – even if it is only back and white.

FIGURE 13.4: A TABLOID PICTURE FEATURE PAGE: THE GAZETTE 10 OCTOBER 2002

Double page spread, monochrome, tabloid

This spread comes from a regional newspaper (*The Gazette*, Blackpool). The page is split into three main sections: the leader column on the left takes two columns under the masthead with a traditional serif font splitting the text. The text is run across the two columns and is set ragged right. This has a tendency to put more white space between the leader column and the rest of the text, making the split more obvious.

The piece on the right is an opinion column but this time the whole thing is laid on a tone patch to draw it away from the rest of the page. The column is run in two columns of ragged right setting under a light heading and a logo.

The main part of the page is taken up with a feature on trains. Not the most promising material as far as pictures go, but the designer still manages to fill almost half the space available with pictures and display material.

The main structure is a large black patch (the whole page is monochrome) spread across the two pages with the main picture pasted onto it. The headline then pierces this main picture taking up the wasted space of the platform and directing the eye to the train and the prominent landmark of Blackpool tower, confirming

Figure 13.4a *The Gazette* (Blackpool) 10 October 2002 page 12

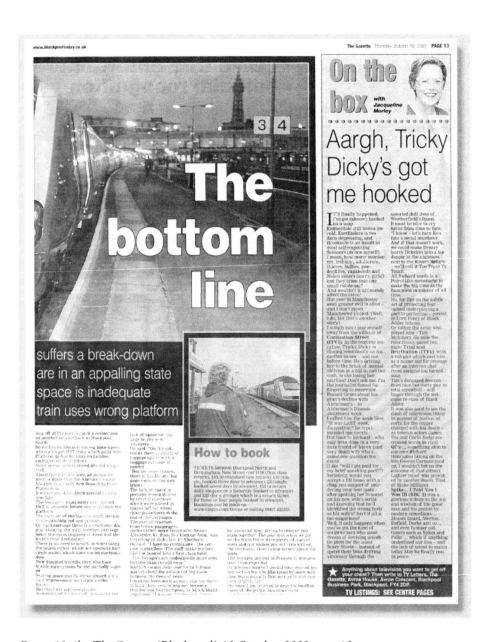

Figure 13.4b   The Gazette (Blackpool) 10 October 2002 page 13

for readers that that is where the picture was taken. The heading is outlined in black to firm up the white and make it easier to read.

The lower part of the black patch is used for a secondary heading that is a list of blob pars about problems with the train. This throws the headline meaning into sharp relief, implying that the railways are under-funded.

The entry point for the story is highlighted by the byline standfirst leading into a drop cap and larger text. The text runs over a fairly wide measure (15 ems) but changes width at several points to allow for the other pictures to cut into the text. Captions are straightforward, running under the pictures.

For the price of a return ticket to Birmingham, *The Gazette* has produced an interesting commentary on the rail system that gets a bold and attractive display. Entry points are clearly signposted and the reader is drawn into the page from the right-hand side with the picture spread and the inserted headline providing a clear signal to grab the reader as they flick through.

FIGURE 13.5: A TABLOID ENTERTAINMENT PAGE: THE GAZETTE, 14 OCTOBER 2002

Right-hand page, monochrome, tabloid

This nicely balanced entertainments page is also from *The Gazette* (Blackpool). It has a titlepiece, as it is the first page of an entertainments supplement. The whole page is in monochrome and the heavy title piece is quickly balanced by the single column profile of Vin Diesel on the right and the tone patch of the review of the previous night's television at the bottom. The space between these is filled with a profile of a new programme. This is a straightforward modular approach, splitting the page into four parts. But good design prevents these four sections splitting way and keeps the page balanced and held together as a cohesive whole.

The main story has an entry point right at the top of the page under the titlepiece. Rather than compete with this, the heading is laid to the right of the intro, above the main picture. The text is run ragged right with the first two paragraphs in larger type. A drop cap marks the entry point. The picture is used at a reasonable size and has a small portrait cut into the top left-hand corner where there is space. The caption is run over the picture alongside the inset oval picture. The headings are set in a strong bold sans serif font and the body type is a typical serif, apart from the profile which is sans serif. This neat, well-balanced page carefully avoids the traps set by the dominating title piece and the need to get some standard material on the page.

Figure 13.5   The Gazette (Blackpool) 14 October 2002 page 13

FIGURE 13.6: SPORTS PAGE: THE GAZETTE, 10 OCTOBER 2002

Left-hand page, monochrome, tabloid

This is an inside sports page that is typical of many regional papers. Most of the page looks at local amateur football, much of it youth football league. The difficulty of finding a lead is often the problem with this sort of sports page. While running reports (usually sent in by club secretaries) of youth and other amateur games is important and draws in a lot of readers, it is often difficult to identify which story should lead the page. In this case, the sub has drawn together a number of matches in the local youth league and separated the various age groups with crossheadings. The intro is one of the higher scoring games that seems to contain some drama. Having manufactured the lead story by editing together a number of reports, it is then run under a two-line six-column streamer. A four-column picture of one of the teams is run on the page. This type of page often suffers because it is not practical to send out a photographer to a match every week, particularly when that match often turns out to be one of the more boring ones or, worse still, is cancelled. Often papers arrange to take team pictures at the start of the season and then use one team each week so that all local players are featured eventually. This can lead to a less than exciting picture week after week but is at least reliable and safe.

Another picture, action this time, is used on the page. This game is not referred to in the text and only the picture and caption register this 10–0 walk-over. It is not clear whether the picture has been sent in by a supporter.

A small anchorpiece gives results for another league while a story across the top of the page (often called a hamper) ensures that the lead does not make it to the top of the page. This keeps the lead as the obvious entry point to the page because of the picture and streamer heading, but makes sure it does not dominate the page and overstate the lead story. The page is finished off with a neat left hand column separated from the rest of the page by a strong 12pt border. This is a league table for the local bowls. League tables are popular in sports pages but should be considered more widely. They are good ways of presenting figures. By tabulating the columns so that they stand beneath each other in neat rows the reader can quickly scan down to find the teams they are interested in and read the results. This sort of table or tabulation is also useful for figures in articles about tax or personal finance, or any other story that relies on a lot of figures.

The page is held together by adhering strongly to style. This is important in a page like this where a number of reports or short stories are drawn together to make a cohesive page. It is vital that crossheads, entry points, logos and captions adhere to house style so that the reader sees a similarity of approach and is quickly able to grasp the navigation marks to his or her way around the page.

Figure 13.6   The Gazette (Blackpool) 10 October 2002 page 48

FIGURE 13.7: A BROADSHEET PAGE: GUARDIAN 11 OCTOBER 2002 PAGE 5

Right-hand page, monochrome, broadsheet

Broadsheet pages tend to be the mark of a more serious paper – one that takes its readers more seriously and intends to give more information and more 'intellectual nourishment'.

This page uses one main story – about celebrity cooking writer and novelist Prue Leith's speaking at the opening of the Institute for Leadership and Management in London, alongside a column of nibs (news in brief).

The nibs are listed under a heading 'In brief'. This is placed on a tone patch that has considerable depth, compared with the type. It has the effect of giving the column depth and standing the nibs away from the main story. The nibs are all run with two-line headings in the *Guardian*'s distinctive sans serif heading font. The body of the nibs is set ragged right, giving a distinctive edge to the page.

The main story concerns Prue Leith claiming that it is the 'kick-ass' style of management in British catering that is driving would-be chefs out of the profession. The *Guardian* draws in quotes from several famous British chefs including Gordon Ramsey, famous for his abrasive style, to make a lively sidebar piece.

The main picture is of Gordon Ramsey in his kitchen and this is 294 sq cm. This means the picture takes 29 per cent of the available space and 36 per cent of the space allocated to that story. Despite this, the picture does not look too big, although it does dominate the page and draws the reader in. This effect is accentuated by the pictures and built-in captions alongside. These make the total graphic area 413 sq cm, or almost exactly 50 per cent of the space allocated to that story. The graphic area, it has to be pointed out, does contain some text. There are short pieces about three of the celebrity chefs mentioned in the story, but they have been cleverly included with the pictures by placing them on a tone background to make them part of the graphics rather than the text. There is also a picture of Prue Leith alongside two quotes which also pull away from the text. Including these and the headline, we can see that the text is in fact the smaller part of this story's display at only 27 per cent of the total space allocated.

The main heading is a single line of sans serif of relatively modest size. It is not the heading that acts as the entry point but the block of graphics beneath it. The main picture here contains plenty of context. Just a momentary glance is enough to gain the impression that the story must be about kitchens or cooks. The main picture is of Gordon Ramsey and many *Guardian* readers will recognise this well-known chef from his TV appearances. Those who don't will easily pick

Figure 13.7 A broadsheet news page. *Guardian* 11 October 2002

up the message from the heading: 'Cook gives celebrity chefs a roasting'. The picture is presumably a library shot (which could have been noted in the caption) as the text says Ramsey is in Dubai. The other pictures are placed on the tone patch with the sidebar material describing their 'bad boy' exploits of the sort that were criticised by Prue Leith in her talk. The font used for this patch is a sans serif, with the heading in a dark grey over the light grey background. The sans serif font is more legible, but probably not as readable. However the sidebar material is only about 200 words long and *Guardian* readers would not find this too fatiguing.

The standfirst, a single strapline under the picture and beneath a broken rule, leads straight into the byline and then the story. It is set in a seriffed font that sets it apart from the lead heading. The kicker face, set light rather than bold, makes it easier to read this streamer heading. The body text is run across four equal columns of 12½ ems in the *Guardian*'s standard seriffed body text. Although the intro paragraph is not signalled with a larger font, there is a large drop cap

– even larger than the main heading font size. No other devices are used to break the text, but with four equal legs (columns), no more than 10 cm long, extra devices are unnecessary. The *Guardian's* readership is intelligent, well-educated and knowledgeable. They will have no trouble reading approximately 1,000 words in a four column block.

It is a neat and well structured page. The nibs are separated by a ½pt rule but they ensure that the story count for the page is high, despite two large 25 cm deep adverts at the bottom of the page. The block of type prevents the page becoming too busy and none of the headings are over-obtrusive. There is a balance about the page that maintains reader interest and ensures they will read the article, or at least start to read it. At the end of the day, it is the quality of the report that will decide whether they bother finishing.

FIGURE 13.8: MAGAZINE NEWS PAGE: COMPUTER SHOPPER, NOVEMBER 2002

Double page, full colour, A4

This is a page from a computer consumer magazine. It runs a number of news pages covering mainly product news. The A4 pages contain stories that are all of about the same strength of interest to the reader. Choosing a lead tends to be almost arbitrary and therefore none gets a particularly big display. The generic header 'Newsfile 11.02' showing the date in a form that mimics computer software protocols is the largest display font on the page. The same sans serif font is used throughout all the headings except for 'CTX kills dead pixel' which is set in a modern serif font to act as a kicker. This is carefully boxed off with a red border under the heading 'Graphics world'. The body font used throughout is also a sans serif font, but it is different to the heading font and is less stylised, more condensed and easier to read.

Despite the apparently haphazard look to the page, it is laid out in clear blocks of material. The page is prevented from being quartered by the addition of the 'in brief' column placed on a black patch staggered across the two facing pages. The crossheads here are in yellow, making them highly visible. The story count, once the nibs are included is high for a relatively small page: nine on the left-hand page, seven on the right.

This gives a busy feel to the pages that is emphasised by the minimalist use of pictures and graphics. Although there are several pictures and graphics on the page, none of them are large and they are used almost exclusively to break the text rather than act as entry points. None of the stories on this page are designed to grab the reader's attention. It is assumed, with the relatively small page size,

Figure 13.8 A magazine news page. *Computer Shopper* November 2002 pages 186 and 187

that the reader is likely to be able to scan the page and quickly zoom in on the displayed headings even though they are not dominant. Colour is used sparingly, although it is available, with the advert for the publication's own website being the most colourful item on the page, apart for the 'Graphics World' story.

The text is place ragged right and most of the headings are single line. This allows for plenty of white space so the overall effect is of a clean tidy and easy to access page, but one that is also busy and packed full of interest.

FIGURE 13.9: A SMALL SCALE MAGAZINE FASHION PAGE: GLAMOUR, OCTOBER 2002

Left-hand page, full colour, 17 cm × 22.5 cm

Glamour is one of the new small scale magazines that have come on the market recently. With a page of 17 cm × 22.5 cm, these are only slightly larger than A5 and are designed to fit easily into a handbag or pocket. Pagination tends to be high, the October 2002 issue that is used here is 370 pages. Although this size is about two-thirds the normal magazine size, it would be interesting to discover if the average reader feels cheated in any way. By use of smaller pictures and display headings each page manages to be a replica of those of larger competitors, giving the impression that the same amount of material goes on each page, but that there are almost double the number of pages. The size seems to be popular and the October 2002 issue contains an editor's letter boasting about Glamour's success 'With 520,000 readers every month, we are far and away the most popular, best-selling women's mag in Britain.'

The page chosen is headed 'The Glamour Challenge'. A twin deck heading quickly sets the scene that this is accessible fashion that the reader can buy in her lunch hour.

The page does not waste space. The models are cut off at the neck by the caption describing the event the outfit is chosen for. So economical is the writing and design, that it takes me more words to describe the text than there are words on the actual page. The pictures of the outfits are large – most of the depth of the page is used by these pictures, but cleverly, those all important accessories with their small details are enlarged and placed over the models' feet. Small captions are inset on shadowed labels giving price and stockist and there is a total cost placed at the bottom of each of the four columns.

This is a page that knows what it is doing and gets right down to it, cutting out all the frills and ruthlessly removing everything that is not needed. The reader wants to know what the page is about – they are told within 3 cm of the top of the page. They want to see what the outfits look like so most of the page is used

Figure 13.9 Fashion page in *Glamour* October 2002 page 224

to show them, with enlargements of what would otherwise be difficult to see detail on shoes, handbags and earrings. The captions are relatively unobtrusive, placed in spaces that do not carry much information. There is a small caption down the inside of the page naming the stylist and photographer and explaining where to find details of the stockists. The captions themselves carry a minimum of information – price and stockist, but it is all most readers need. The page is in full colour (as are all the pages in *Glamour*) so the reader can see the colours for herself. It is assumed that if the reader is interested, she will be happy to visit the shop and see the outfit for herself so telling her details about materials, sizes, alternate colours and so on are clearly seen as a waste of space – and there is no space to waste on a page this small. The colours used on the page blend well with the outfits. The left-hand dress is bright red and the skirt and top outfit alongside are a deepish orange. The other outfits are black, apart from the jeans which are a typical blue. The column headers and footers are mixed in dark orange or light orange and these colours are also used in the heading. These colours brighten the black outfits and accentuate the colours.

All in all it is a well-put-together, cleverly-thought-through page. It wastes no space and presents the reader with exactly what she needs. According to *Glamour* (October 2002: 13), the magazine won the Total Publishing Awards 2001 for Best Designed Consumer Magazine, and, if this edition of the magazine is a good example, it deserved it.

Glossary

Advertising feature: Editorial copy and pictures that are produced to support an advert or series of adverts.
Ampersand: Special character (&) to represent the word 'and'.
Anchorpiece: Story placed at the bottom of a page to hold it together.
Anti-aliasing: Smoothing the rough, pixilated edges of pictures produced in a digital process.
Ascender: Top portion of letters b, d, f, h, k, l.

Bastard setting: Any measure that deviates from the normal.
Beard: The non-printing portion of type which coincides with descenders on characters that have descenders.
Black: Bold-faced text type.
Bleed: Allowing a picture to extend beyond the trimmed area of a page.
Block: Engraved or etched plate from which a picture or graphic is printed.
Blurb: A piece of editorial, usually on the front page, advertising a story within.
Bold: Thickened, heavier version of roman type.
Broadsheet: Large size newspaper, usually considered to be of a more serious quality.
Byline: Reporter's name given with a printed story.

Caps: Short for capital letters.
Casting off: An estimation of the set length of a piece of copy in a given type size and measure.
Catchline: One-word name used to identify a story set in type – should be removed before publication.
Centre spread: Two facing pages in the middle of a newspaper or magazine.
Chase: The metal frame that held metal type for printing.
Cicero: European measure of type.
CMYK: Short for process colour, representing the four colours used: cyan, magenta, yellow and black.
Condensed: A type which is narrow for the family from which it comes giving a better word count.
Copy approval: Allowing the subject of a story to read the copy and have approval over whether it is published.
Copy taster: Someone who 'tastes' – approves copy for publication.
Crop: To select an area of a picture for publication and remove the remainder.
Crosshead: Display type sub-heading centred within the body of the story allowing the eye to rest and identify where it is. (See side-head.)

Cut off rule: A line across a column indicating the end of that story.
Cut out: A picture with the background, or part of the background removed to allow it to fit over another picture or to allow text to be wrapped close to the subject.

Deck: Separate section of heading – not separate lines.
Descenders: Bottom portion of letters such as g, p, q, j ,y
Dots per inch: A way of measuring the resolution of scanners and printers. The more dots per inch, the higher the resolution.
Double page spread: Facing pages where the type fills both pages running over the centre gutter.
Drop letter: Initial letter which is large enough to run alongside two or three lines of text. (Also drop cap.)
Dummy: Mock-up of a newspaper showing on which page the adverts are to go and allowing decisions on story placing to be made.

Edition: A version of a publication. Different editions of a publication might be produced daily, weekly or monthly. They might even be produced for different times of the day or different locations such as district, city etc.
Ellipses: Three dots (. . .) indicating a pause or that something is missing.
Em-dash: A dash the size of an em.
Em-quad: The square of the body type. Usually assumed to be a pica-em or a 12pt em. (See also mutton.)
En: Half an em.
Entry point: The starting point on a page for a reader.
EPS: Encapsulated postscript. A digital graphics format.

Face: Short for typeface.
Fair comment: A defence against a defamation suit where it is claimed the comments are fair, based on true facts.
Flong: A cast in papier mâché or plastic of the type set.
Folio: The part of the page that gives the page number.
Font: A complete set of type characters in any size and face.
Footer: The bottom area of the page sometimes used to insert the publication title, date or page number.
Full out: Set right to margins without any indent.
Full point: Another name for a full stop.

Gutter: Space between pages on the same form.

Halftone: Plate of copper and zinc or photographic bromide in which the tonal values of a photograph or picture are represented as dots for printing.
Hanging indent: Where the first line is full out and the rest of the par is indented, usually by one em.

Imprint: The name and address of the printer and publisher which is required by law on any publication.
Intro: The starting paragraph of a story.

Justification: Setting type so that both sides of the text are level.

Keep down: Use only lower case letters.

Keep up: Use caps.

Kern: Part of a letter projecting beyond its body.

Kerning: Adjusting the space between letters in computer typesetting to ensure that different kerns do not leave a displeasing visual effect.

Layout: The page design sent to the printer.

Lead: Pronounce 'leed' The main story on the page. Also the starting point of a story or nose.

Lead: Pronounced 'led' originally strips of metal (lead) which spaced out lines of type. Now the space between lines which is additional to the body size.

Leader: The Editorial comment.

Leaders: A line of dots, dashes or other devices to lead the eye across the page especially in a table.

Leading: Pronounced 'ledding' – the space between lines of type.

Letterpress: A method of printing involving pressing raised, inked type against paper.

Literals: A whole range of printer's errors from spelling mistakes to wrong founts.

Lithography: A method of printing involving the separation of ink and water.

Live page: A page produced on the day it is made up.

Make-up: The sheet on which the design of the page is drawn.

Masthead: The paper's titlepiece. As Leslie Sellers points out in his excellent book, *Doing it in Style*, although this usage has wide currency, it is a misuse. The masthead should *be* the title and other material above the editorial leader.

Measure: The width (always in 12pt ems) to which type is set.

Mutton: A common name for an em.

Negs: Photographic negatives.

Nut: Common name for an en.

Offset: A printing system where the plate is separated from the paper by an offset roller, so that there is no direct contact.

Over matter: Set type in excess of requirements.

Overnights: Pages designed and set up the night before.

Paste-up: The art of putting together a photoset page.

Perfector: A printing machine that allows pages to be printed on both sides.

Pica: The old name for 12pt.

Pierce: Cutting into a picture to allow text, or another picture to be inserted.

Platen: The plate that paper is pressed against during printing.

Play up: Instruction to emphasise a particular story or angle of a story. The opposite is play down.

Point: Standard unit of typographical measurement. Approx 72pts to the inch or 0.01383 inches.

Privilege: A protection against a suit of defamation allowing freedom of speech at public meetings.

Process colour: A method of printing in full colour involving printing in four different coloured inks – also known as CMYK.

Publication: An identifiable journal that is published on a regular basis.

Puff: An advert, often on the front page, telling about material inside the paper or magazine.

Random: The area where type is assembled for proofing and sometimes make-up.

Raster dot: A printing term that allows black ink to be produced in dot screen to represent a shade of grey.

Reader: A corrector of set type.

Register: The exact positioning of one colour in relation to others. Colour printing requires that all four colour plates are in register or the image will be blurred.

Replate: A change of page to include urgent news or correct a major mistake. This would be in addition to a normal plate change for an edition change.

Rule: Lines originally produced with strips of metal but more likely to be photographically produced these days.

Run: The number of copies required in any printing operation.

Shoulder: The angle formed by a change in measure of a story.

Side-head: A display type sub-heading placed within the body of text and aligned with either the right or left side of the text.

Slip: A special page for a specific area or particular audience.

Smalls: Classified ads, but also another name for shorts.

Solus: A single advert on a page.

Spot colour: An additional colour added to a publication during printing.

Spread: Material spread over more than one page and designed as a whole.

Standfirst: A display device that introduces a story, often containing the reporter's byline

Stone hand: A person who puts together a page (also paste-up artist).

Stone sub: A sub who oversees the putting together of pages and approves the finished pages.

Stone: Table on which pages are made up. Originally made of marble. Now more likely to be a make-up or paste-up table. Also used to refer generally to the composing department. 'You'll find Jim up on the stone.'

Strapline: A heading placed over another heading.

Streamer: A long heading, usually covering the full width of the page.

Supplement: A one-off magazine or newspaper insert that is a part of but separate to the main newspaper.

Tasted: As in copy tasted. Copy that has been approved or rejected.

Titlepiece: The title of the publication on the front page.

Widows and orphans: The lonely word or words that fail to fill the last line of a paragraph but have been allowed to move into the next column and sit alone at the top.

WEBSITE OF INTEREST

www.poynter.org

Bibliography

Ang, T. (1996) *Picture Editing*, Oxford: Focal Press

Burnham, R.W., Hanes, R.M. and Bartleson J.C. (1963) *Color: a Guide to Basic Facts and Concepts*, New York: John Wiley and Sons

Carey, P. (1996) *Media Law*, London: Sweet and Maxwell

Carey, P. (2000) *Media Law* (2nd edn), London: Sweet and Maxwell

Cook, A. and Feury, R. (1989) *Type and Color*, Rockport: Rockport Publishers

Craig, J. (1980) *Designing with Type*, New York: Watson-Guptill Publications

Crone, T. (1995) *Law and the Media* (3rd edn), London: Focal Press

De Grandis, L. (1986) *Theory and Use of Colour*, Poole: Blandford Press

Durrant, W.R. (1989) *Printing*, Oxford: Heinemann Professional Publishing

Evans, H. (1978) *Pictures on a Page*, London: William Heinemann

Evans, H. (1984) *Newspaper Design*, London: William Heinemann

Evans, H. (1984) *Handling Newspaper Text*, London: William Heinemann

Favre, J. and November, A. (1979) *Color and Communication*, Zurich: ABC edition

Frost, C. (2000) *Media Ethics and Self-regulation*, London: Pearson

Frost, C. (2001) *Reporting for Journalists*, London: Routledge

Garcia, M. and Stark, P. (1991) *Eyes on the News*, St Petersburg: Poynter Institute

Giles, V. and Hodgson, F.W. (1996) *Creative Newspaper Design* (2nd edn), Oxford: Focal Press

Greenwood, W. and Welsh, T. (2000) *McNae's Essential Law For Journalists* (16th edn), London: Focal Press

Hodgson, F.W. (1993) *Subediting* (2nd edn), Oxford: Focal Press

Hutt, A. (1967) *Newspaper Design* (2nd edn), London Oxford University Press

Kammermeier, A. and Kammermeier, P. (1992) *Scanning and Printing*, Oxford: Focal Press

Keeble, R. (2001) *Ethics for Journalists*, London: Routledge

Kieran, M. (1998) *Media Ethics*, London: Routledge

Kress, G. and van Leeuwen, T. (1996) *Reading Images: The Grammar of Visual Design*, London: Routledge

Kress, G. and Van Leeuwen, T. (2000) 'Front Pages (The Critical) Analysis of Newpaper Layout' in Bell, A. and Garret, P. (eds) *Approaches to Media Discourse*, pp. 186–219 Oxford: Blackwells

Mason, P. and Smith, D. (1998) *Magazine Law: A Practical Guide*, London: Routledge

Press Complaints Commission (1997) Report no 40 London: PCC Press Complaints Commission and (1993) Report no 16 London: PCC

Quinn, S. (2001) *Digital Sub-editing and Design*, Oxford: Focal Press

Quinn, T., Lindsay, M., Hewitt, D., Overbury, K. and Ritson, J. (1991) *The Key: A Guide to Best Practices for Thomson Regional Newspapers*, Belfast: TRN

Sasoon, R. (1993) *Computers and Typography*, Oxford: Intellect

Sellers, L. (1968a) *Doing it in Style*, Oxford: Pergamon Press

Sellers, L. (1968b) *The Simple Subs Book*, Oxford: Pergamon Press

Shipcott, G. (1994) *Typography for Desktop Publishers*, London: B.T. Batsford Ltd

Smith, A. (ed) (1974) *The British Press Since the War*, Newton Abbott: David and Charles

Steinberg, S.H. (1955) *Five Hundred Years of Printing*, Harmondsworth: Penguin

Tinker, M. (1963) *The Legibility of Print*, Ames: Iowa State University Press

Twyman, M. (1970) *Printing 1770–1970: An Illustrated History of its development and uses in England*, London: Eyre and Spottiswood

Weinmann, E. (1998) *QuarkXPress 4 for Windows*, Berkeley: Peachpit Press

Williams, R. (1994) *The Non-designers Design Book*, Berkeley: Peachpit Press

Zelanski, P. and Fisher, M.P. (1989) *Colour for Designers and Artists*, London: The Herbert Press

Index